AN ADULT COLORING BOOK

Mystery Women

by

M.R. Umlas

Illustrated by

Rolando Jimenez

Author/Producer: Maria Roselle G. Umlas
Illustrator: Rolando Jimenez
Cover & Layout Design: Kathleen Melendrez

Printed in the Philippines by VisualTek Graphic Solutions & Pressworks, Co.

She bound her tears in leather
And made them into shoes,
She walked in them for far and wide
Each step a painful one.

Up and down the wavy hills
Across the seas she went,
Until the pair had broken down
And she had found herself.

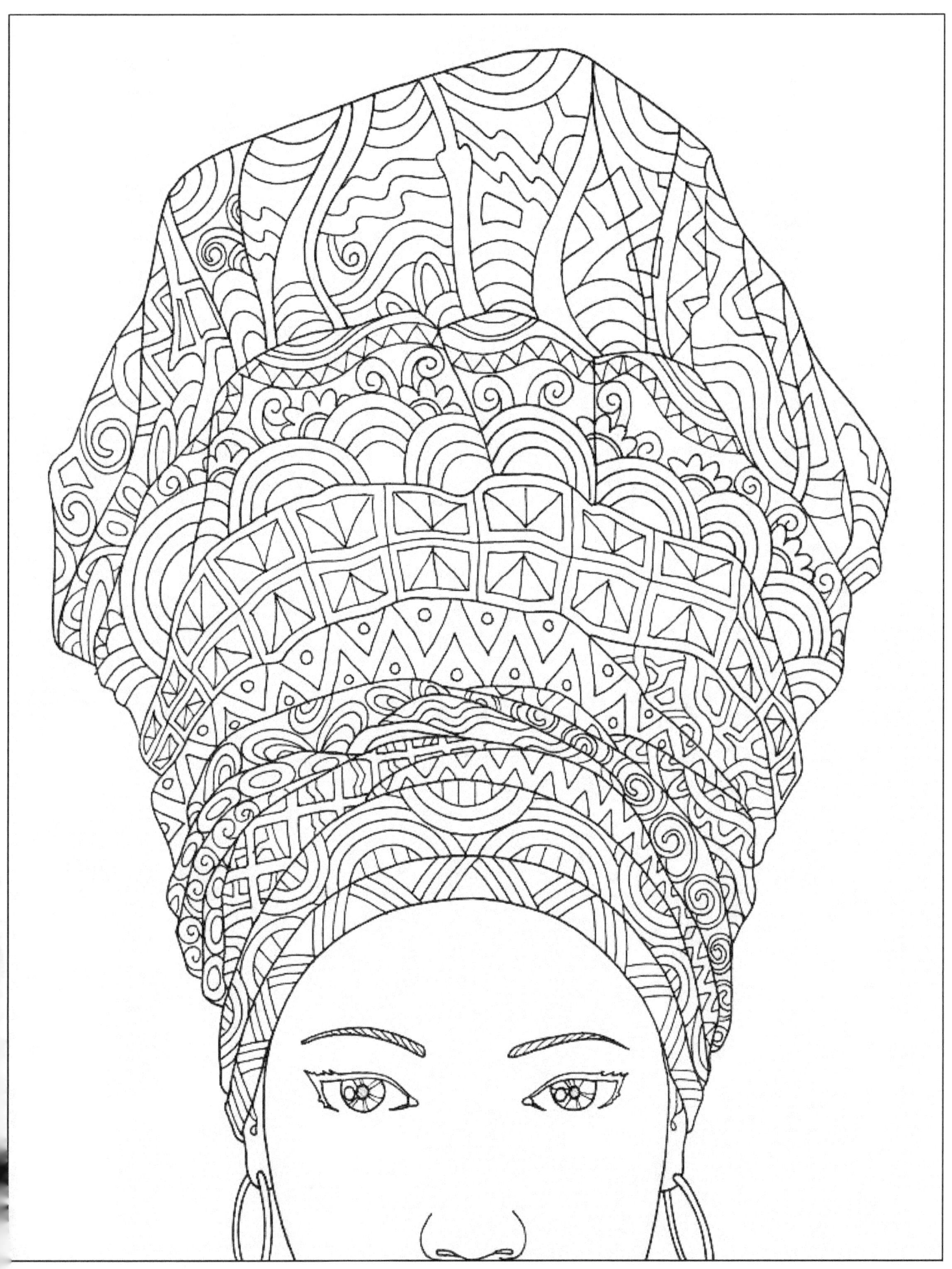

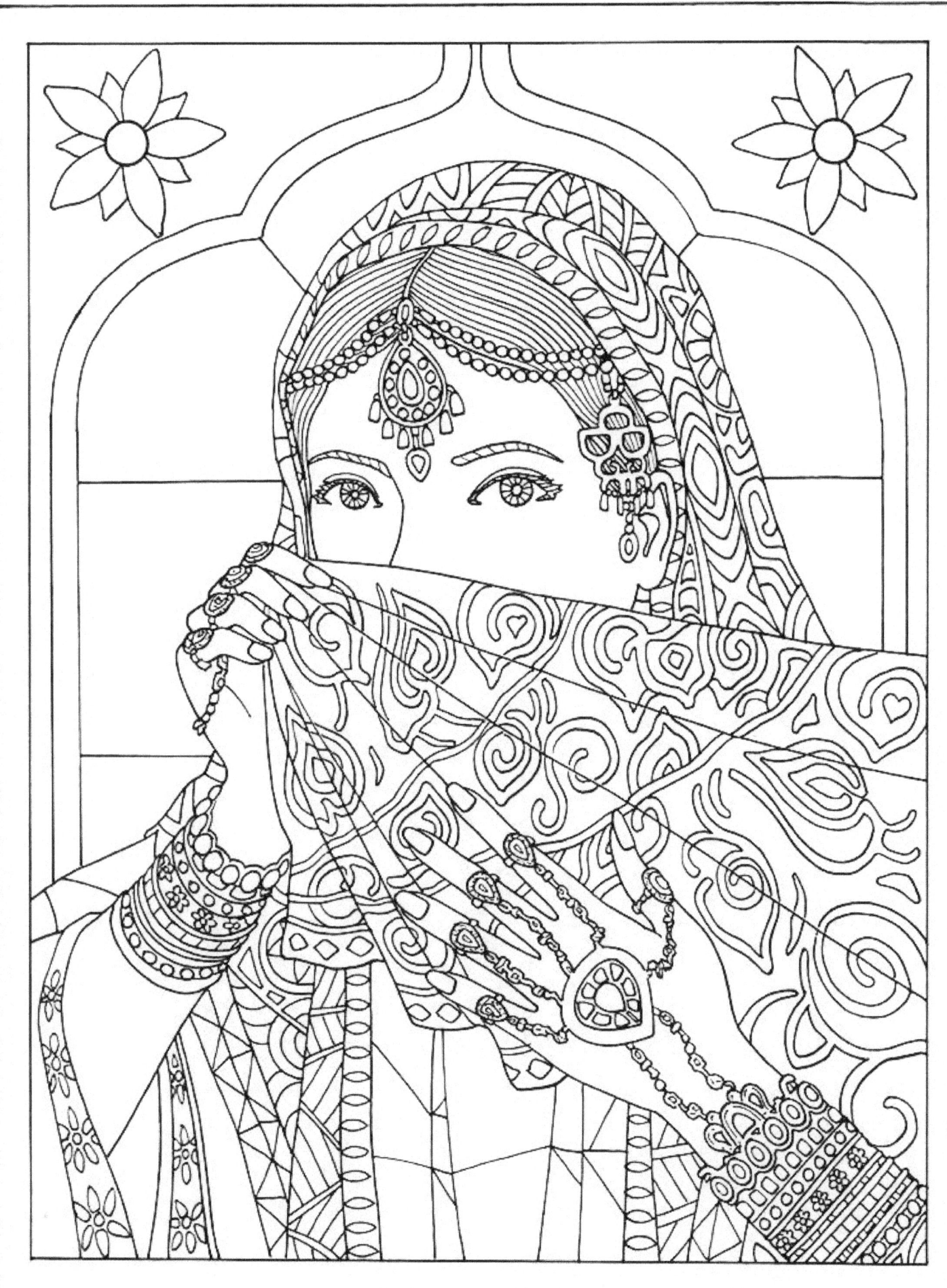

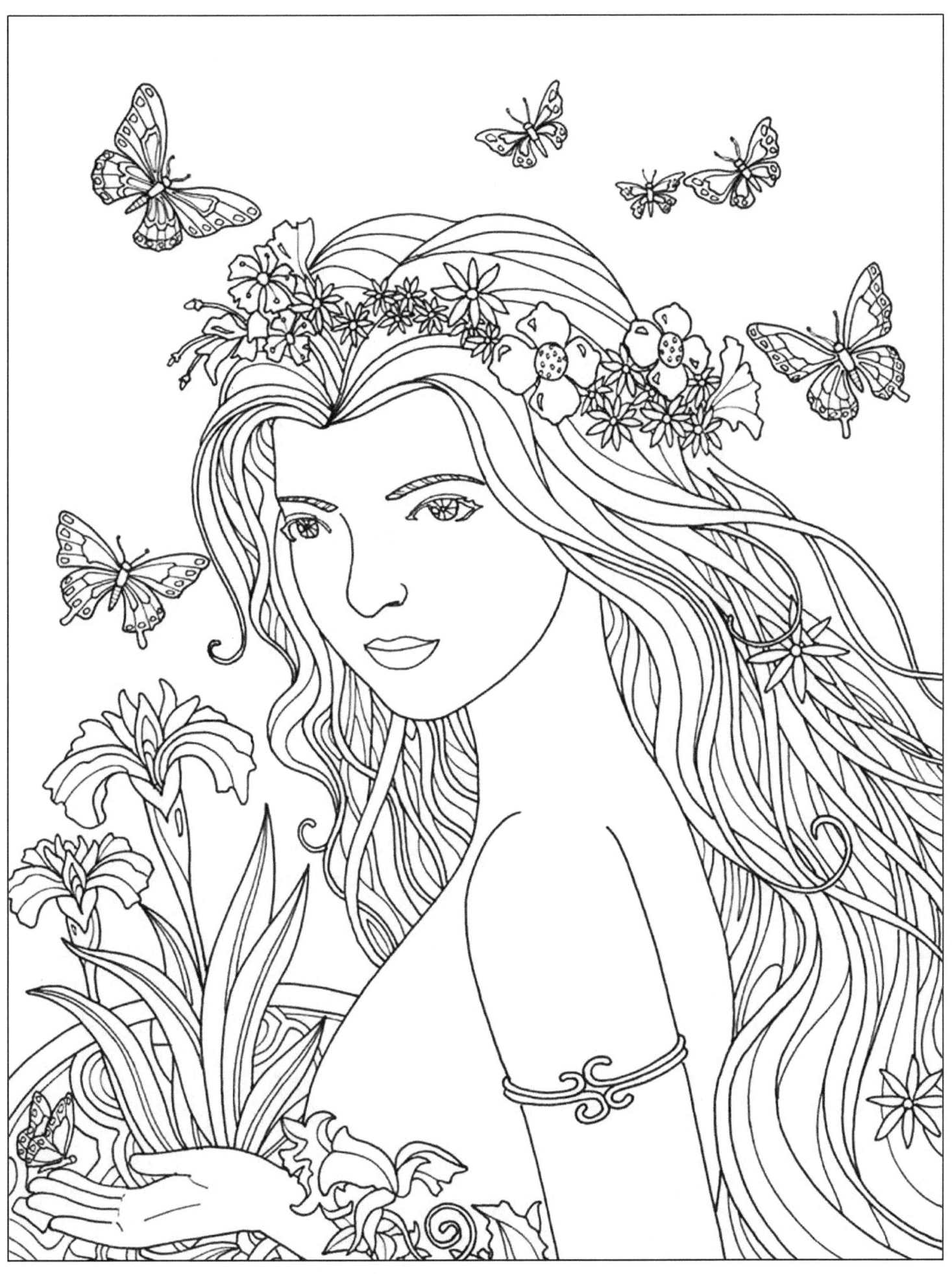

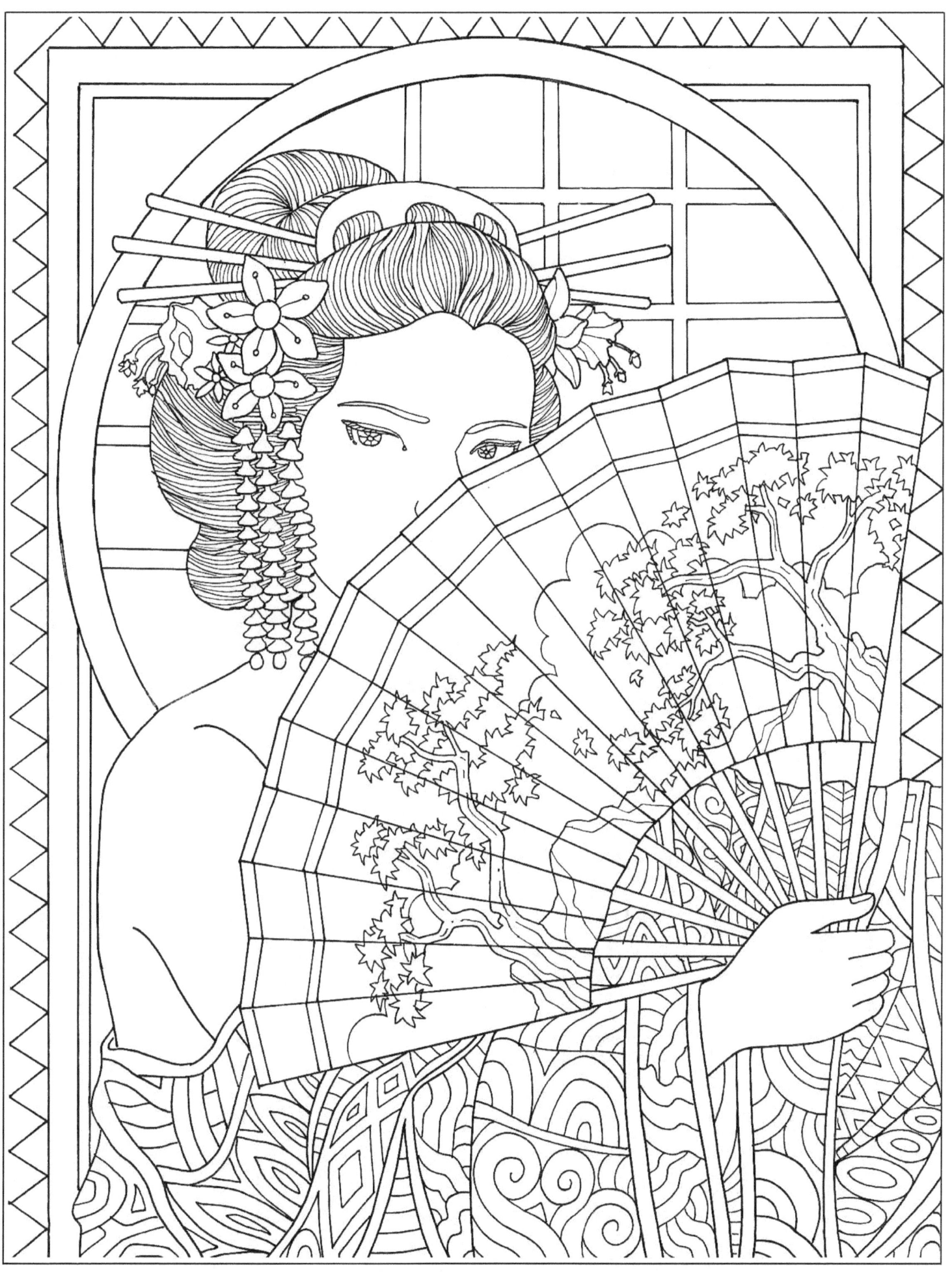

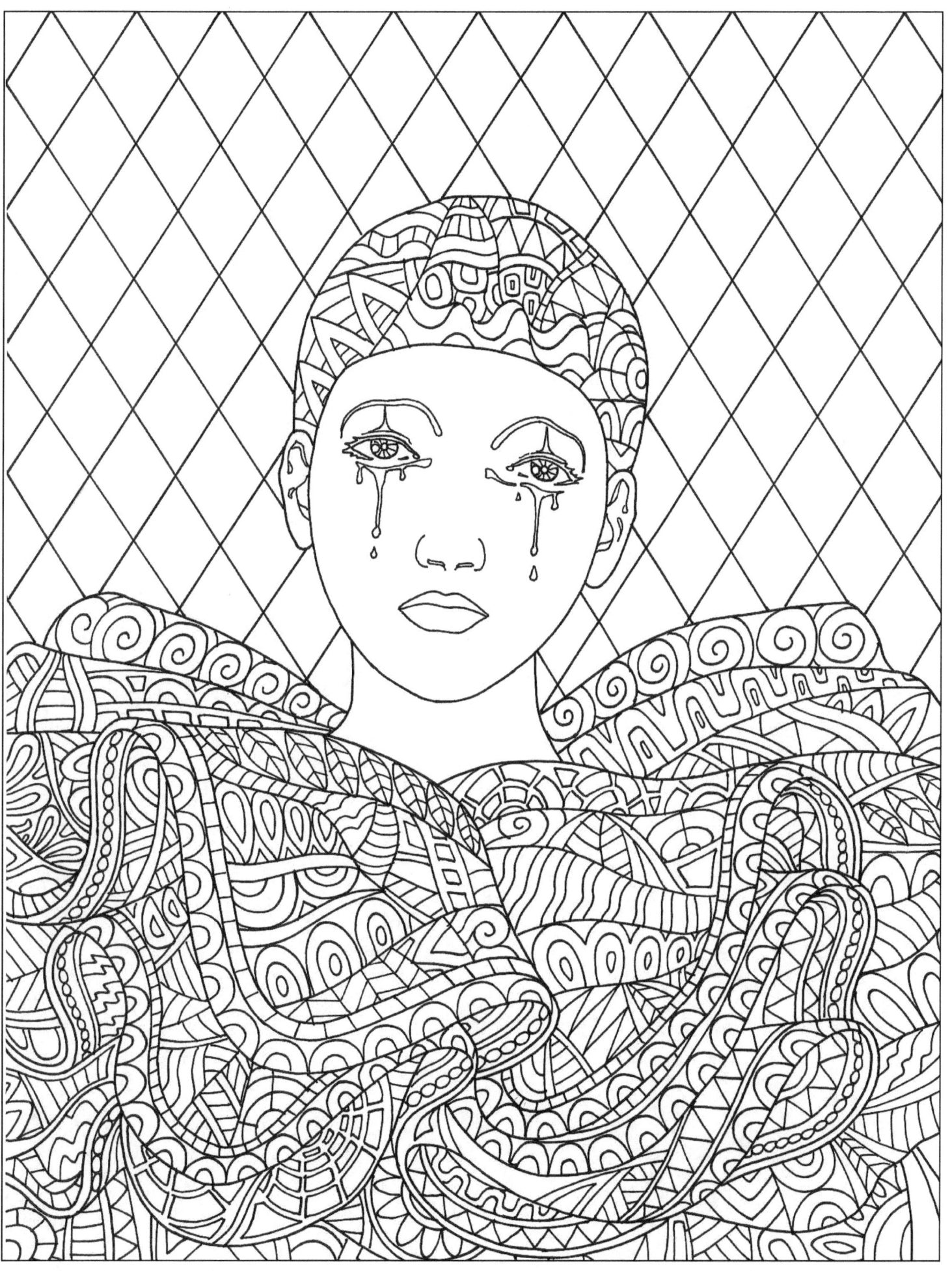

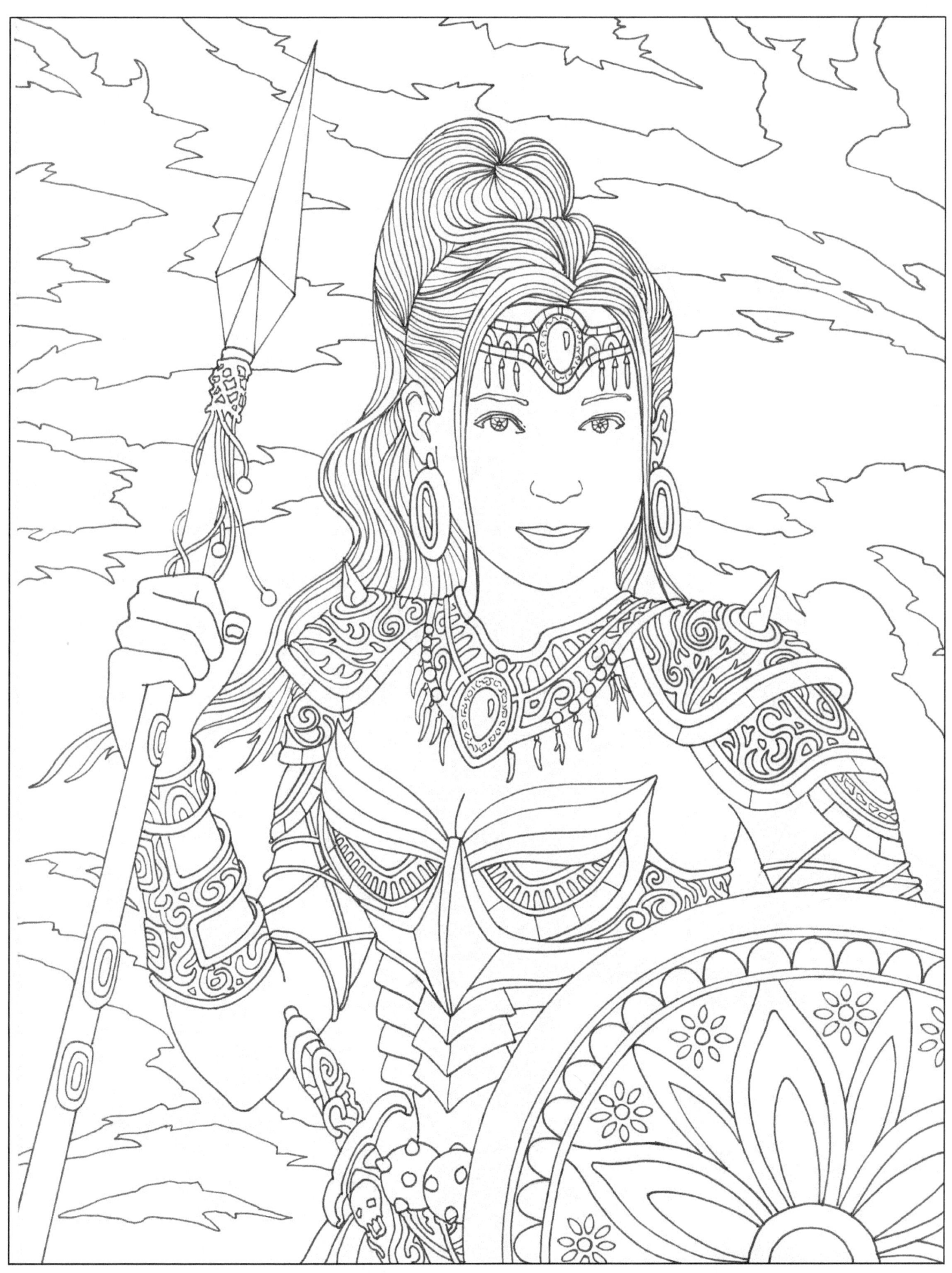

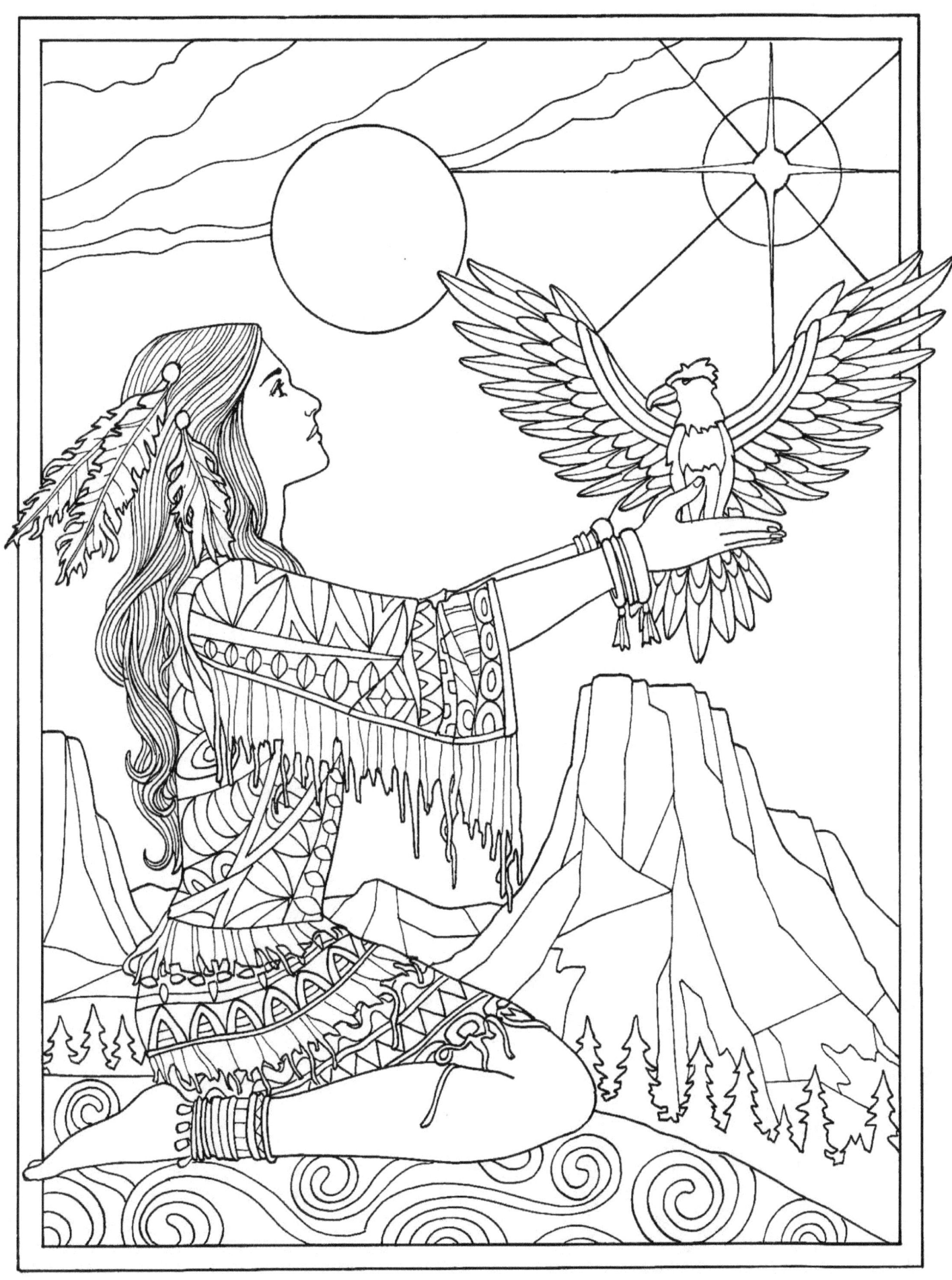

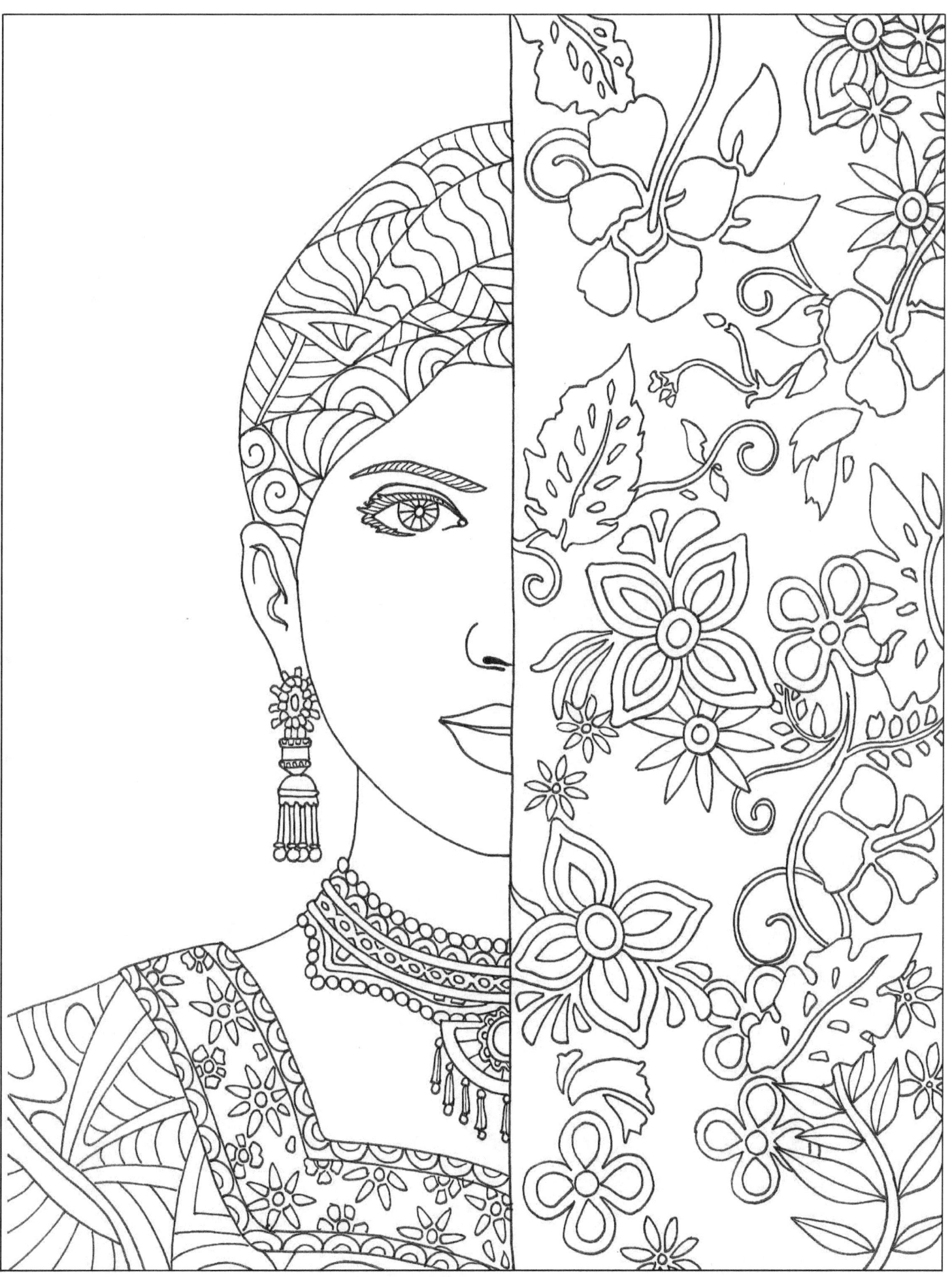

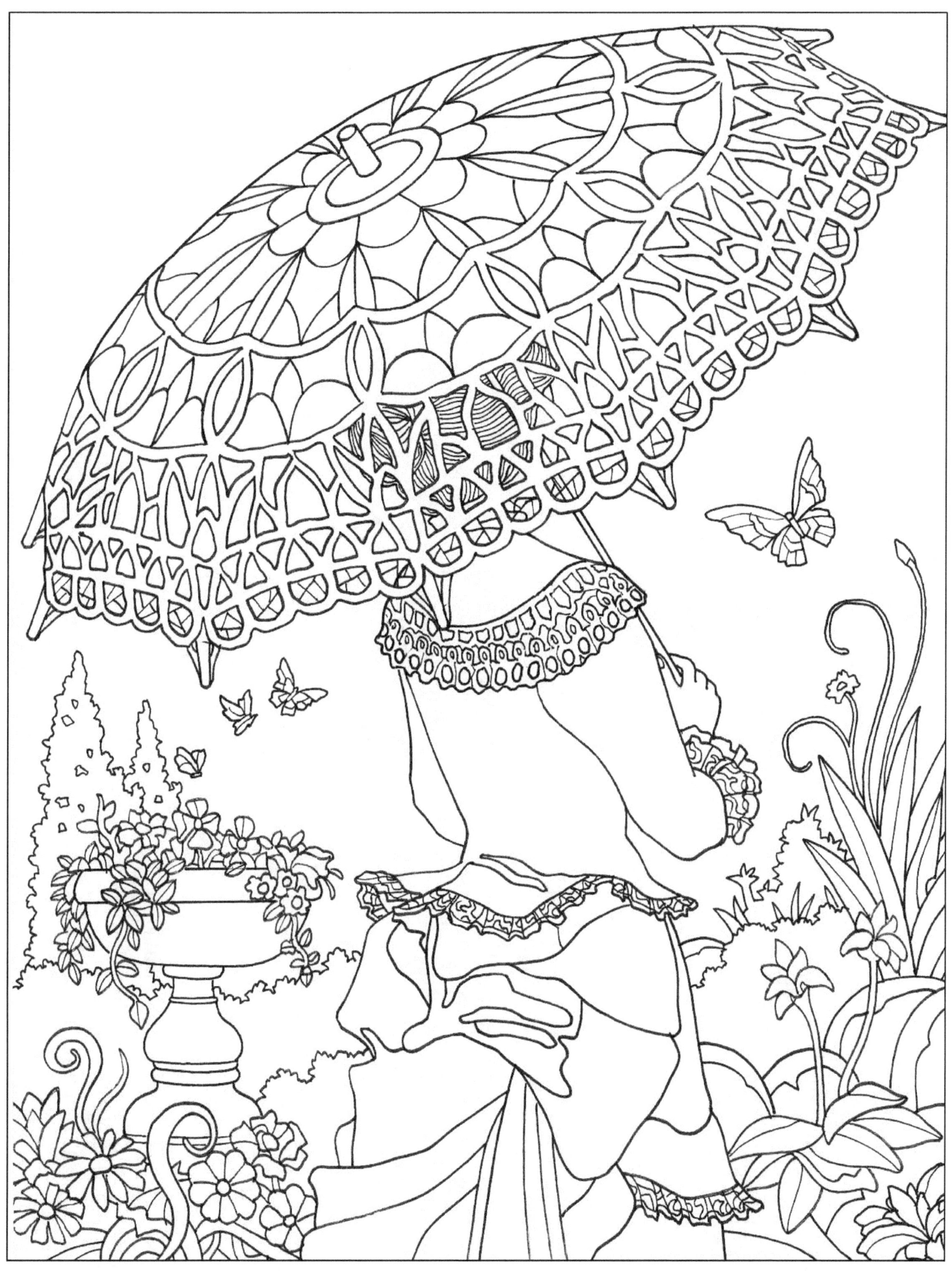

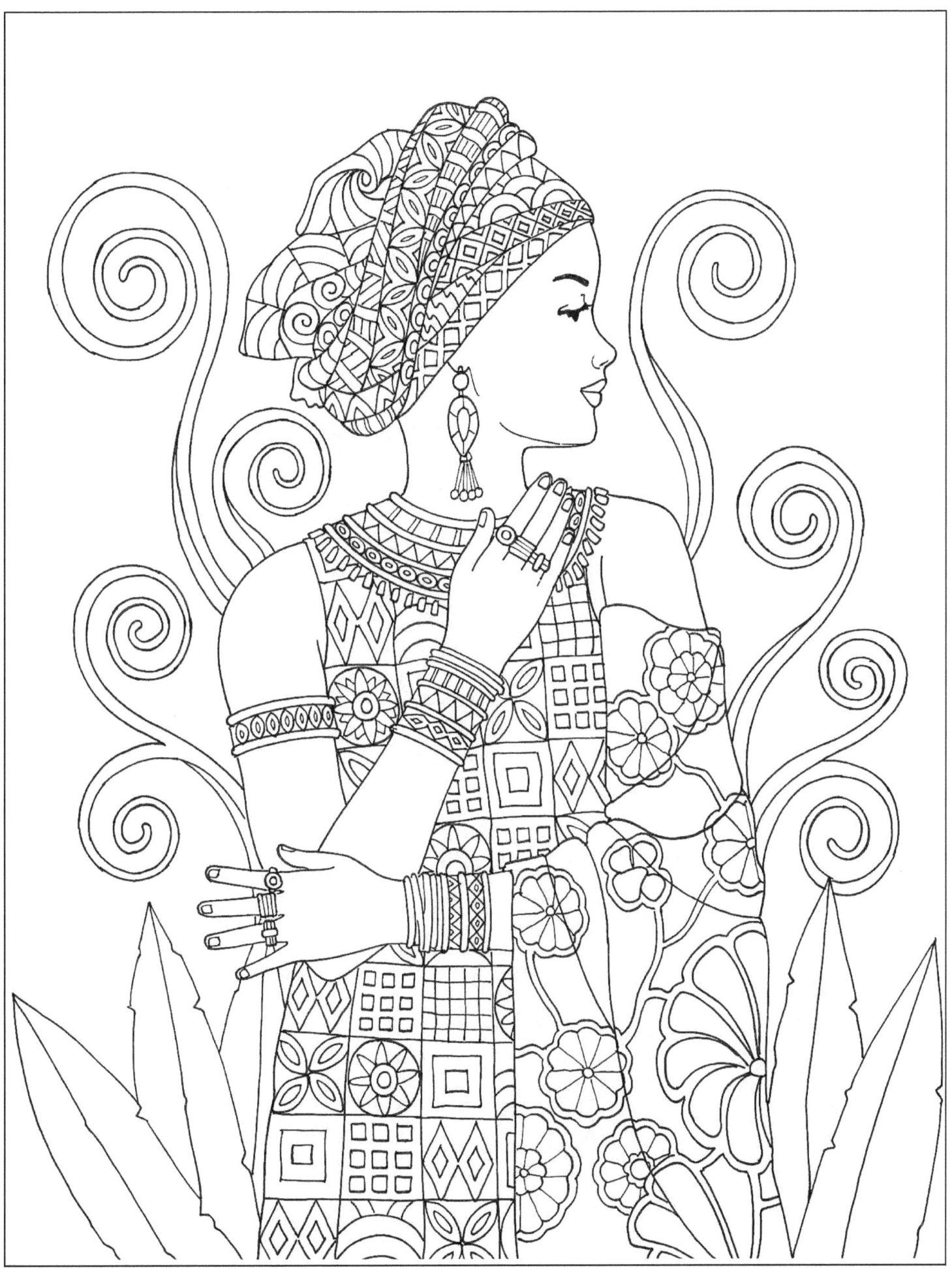

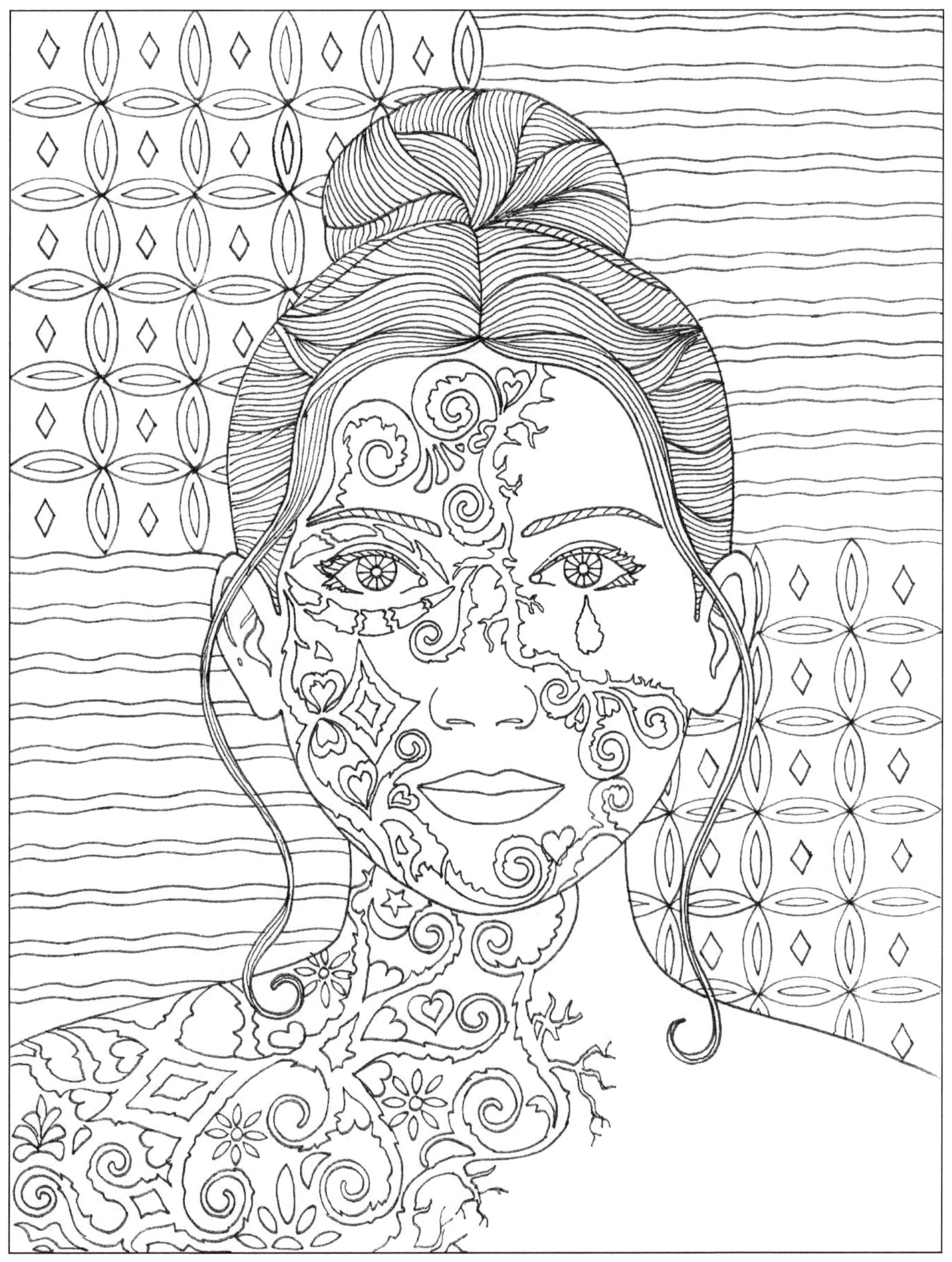

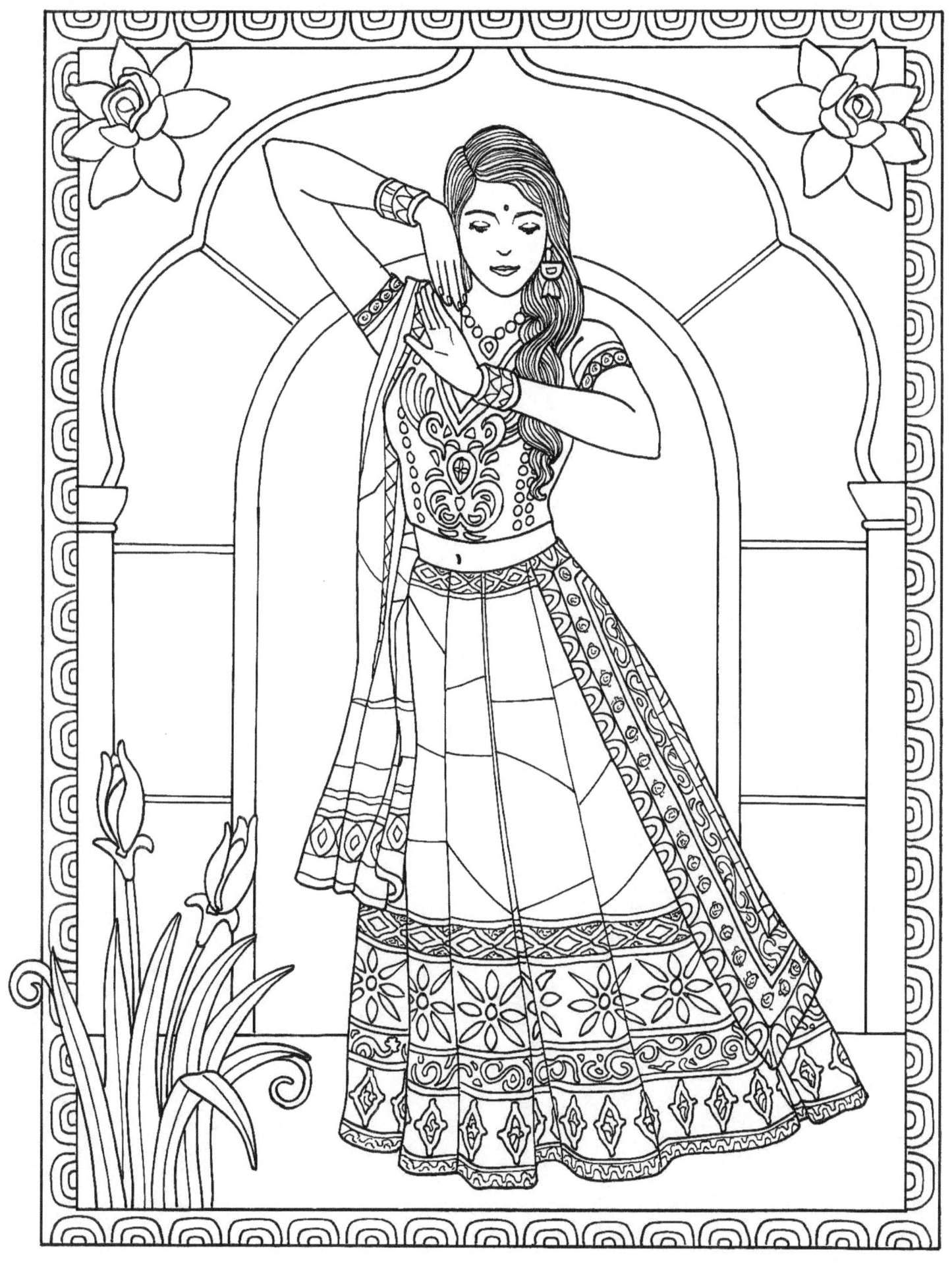

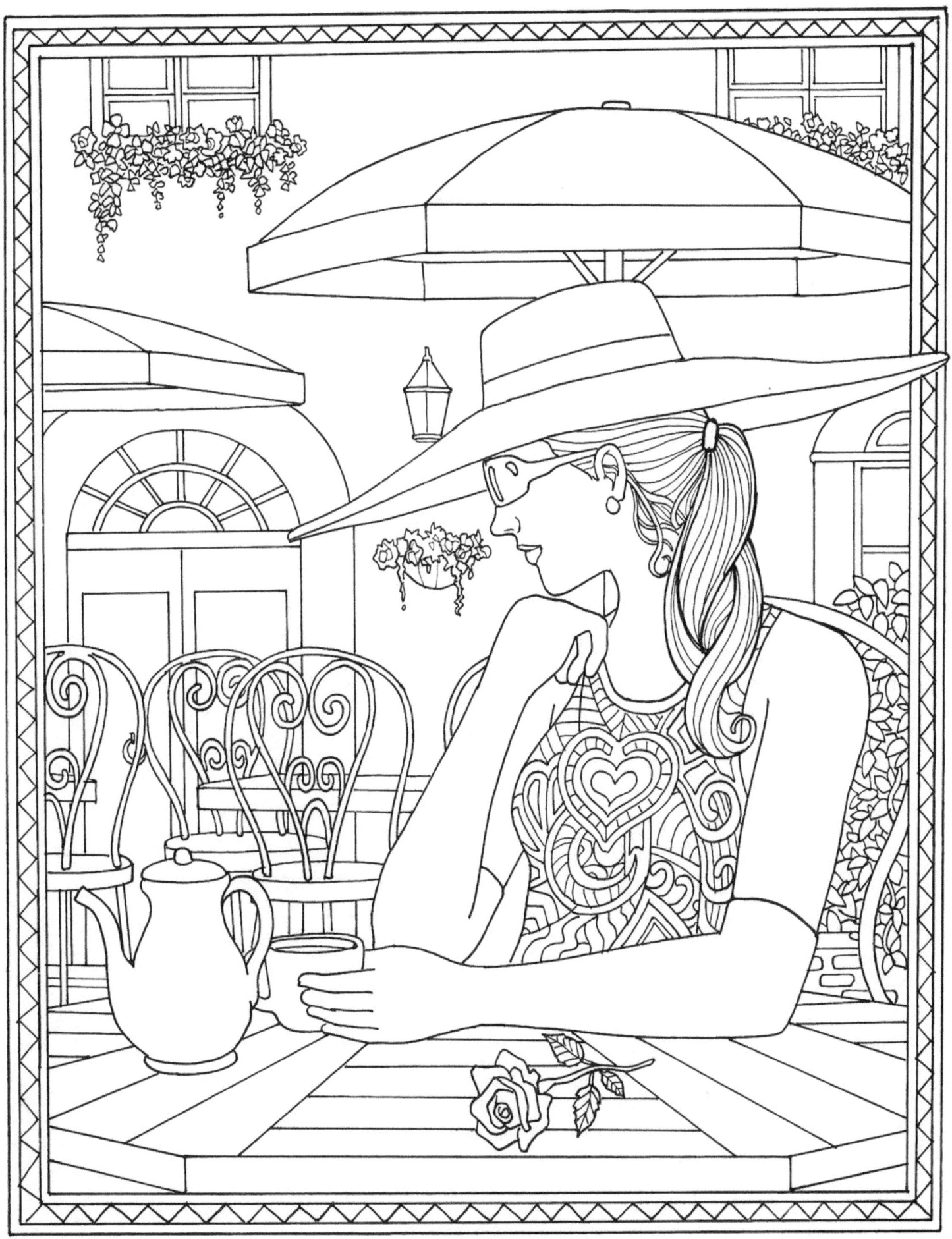

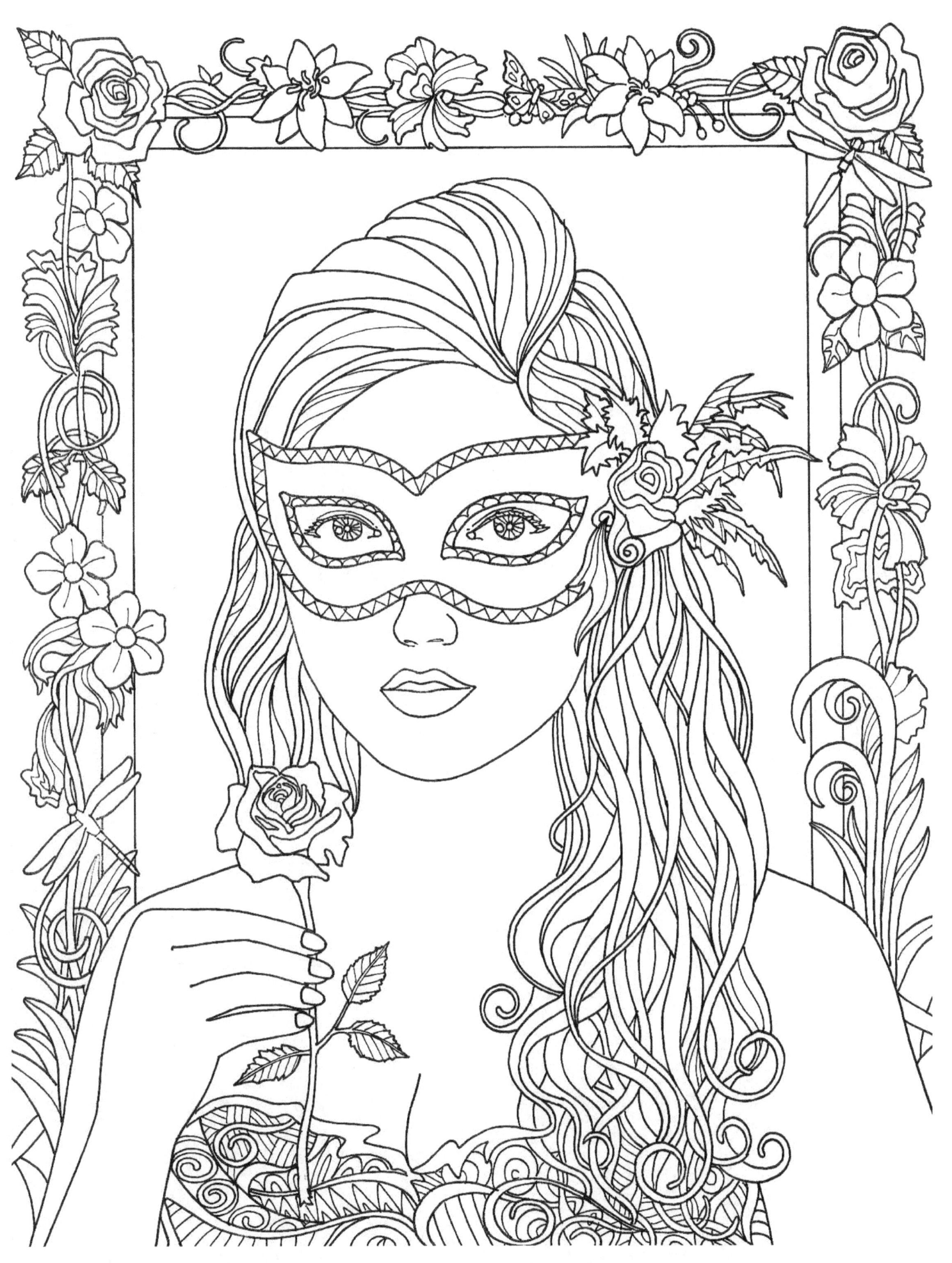

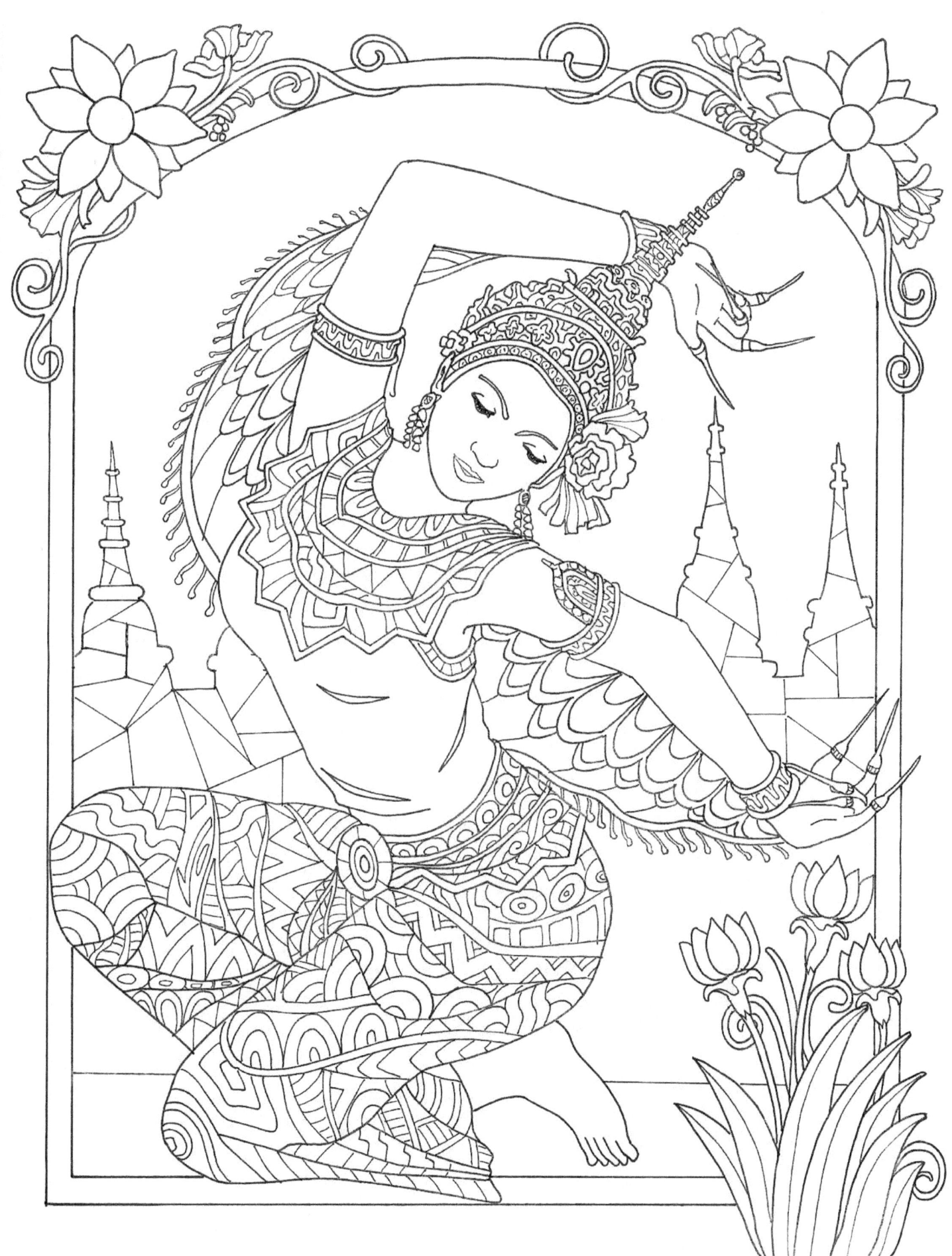

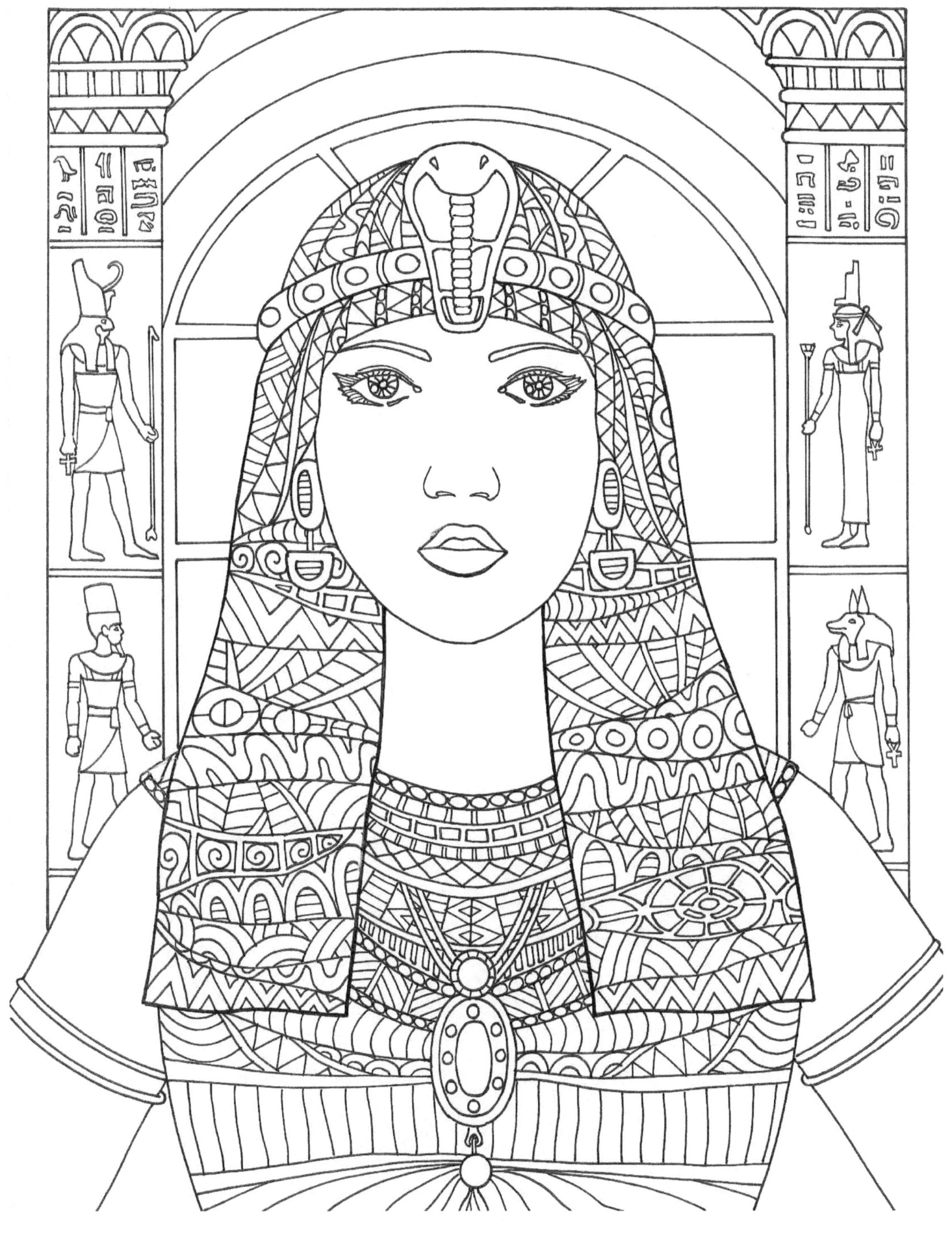

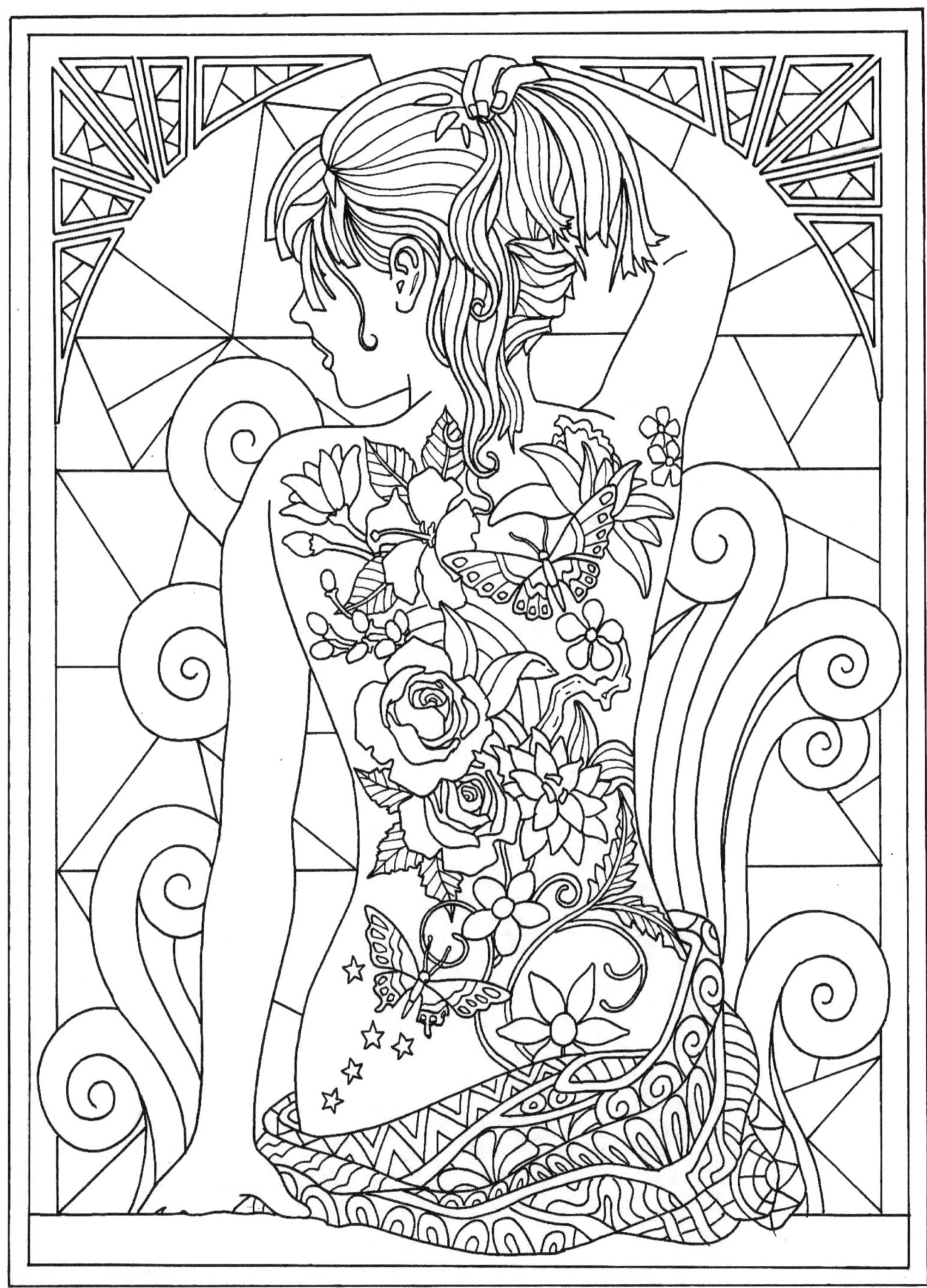

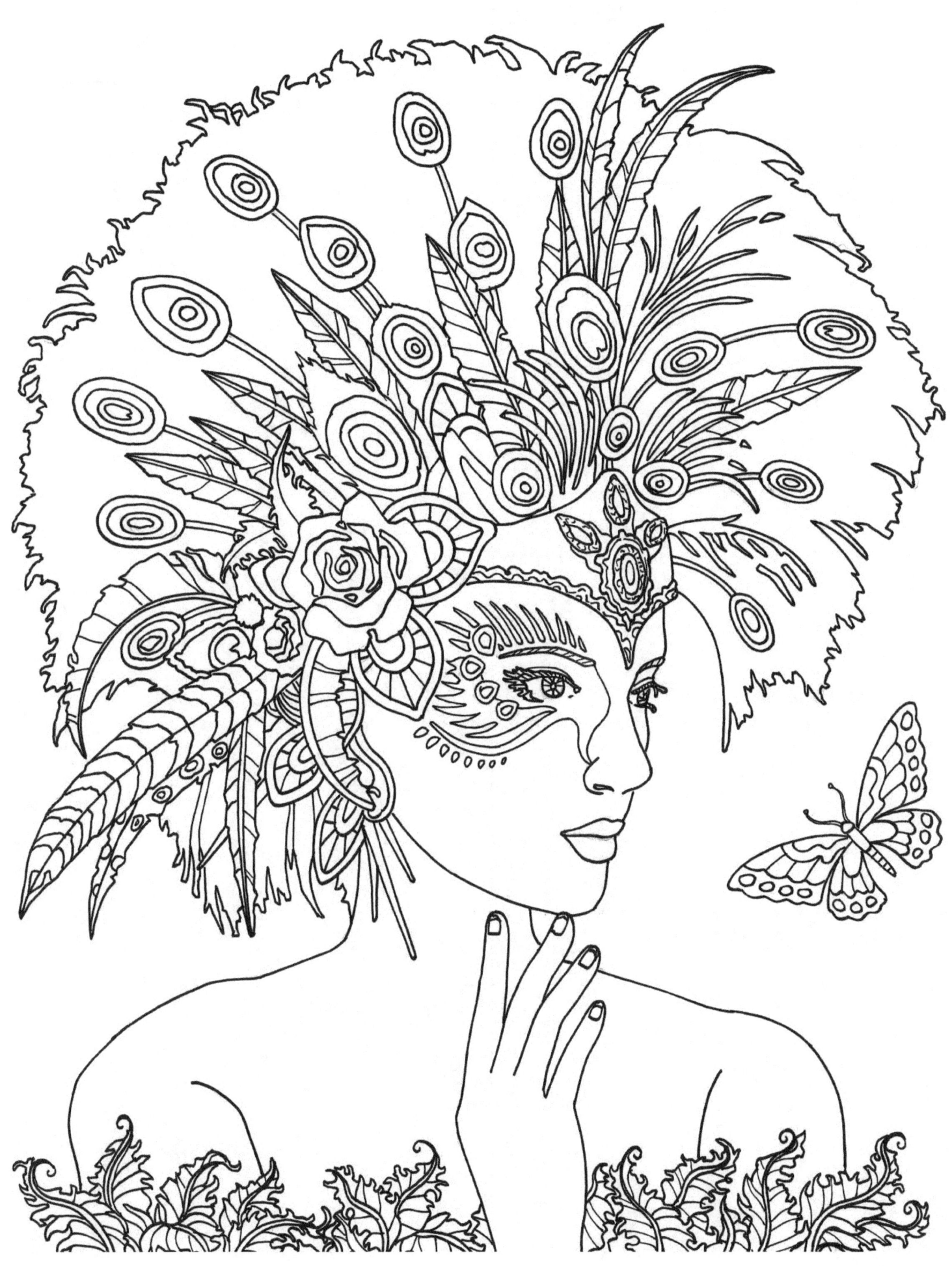

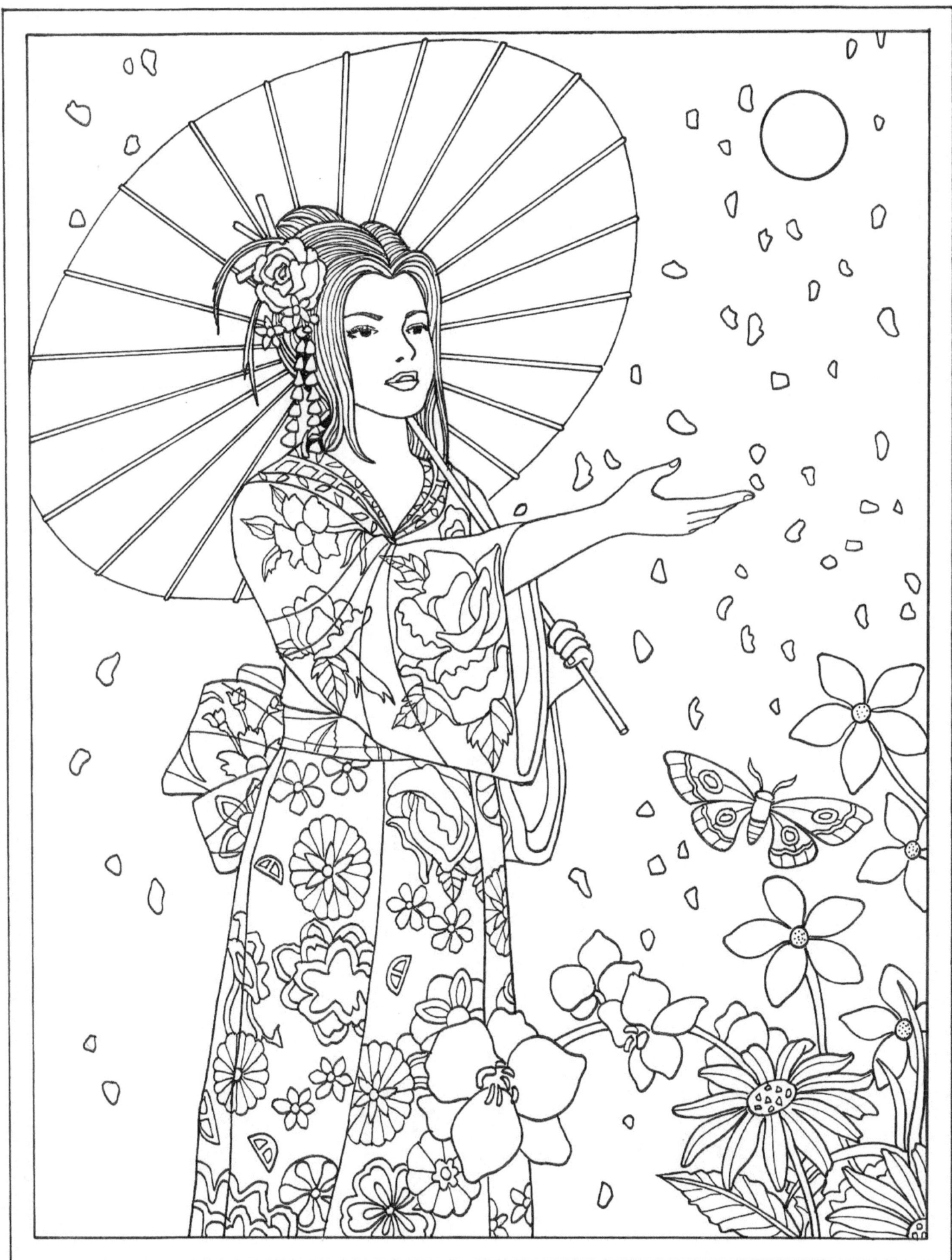

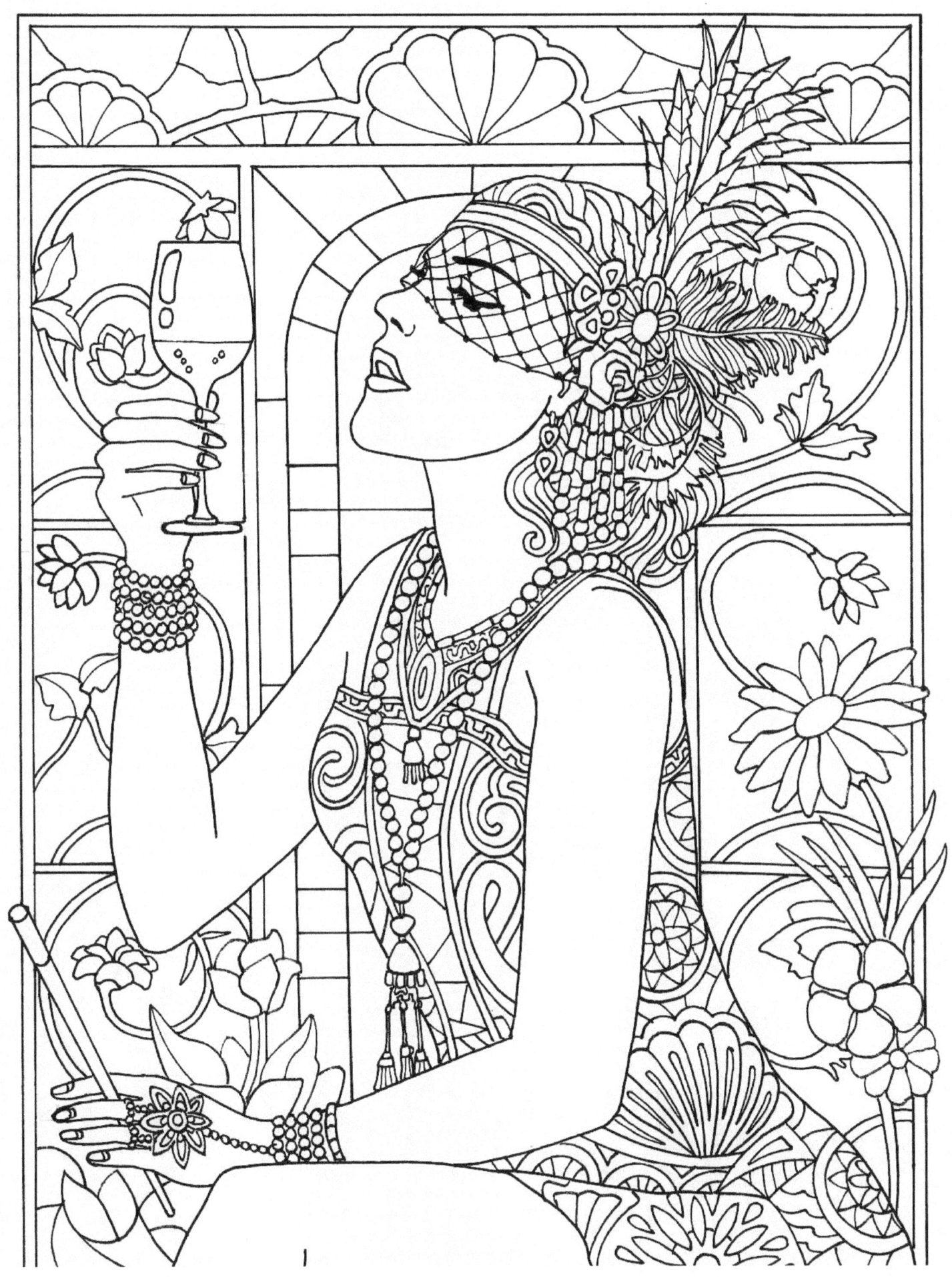

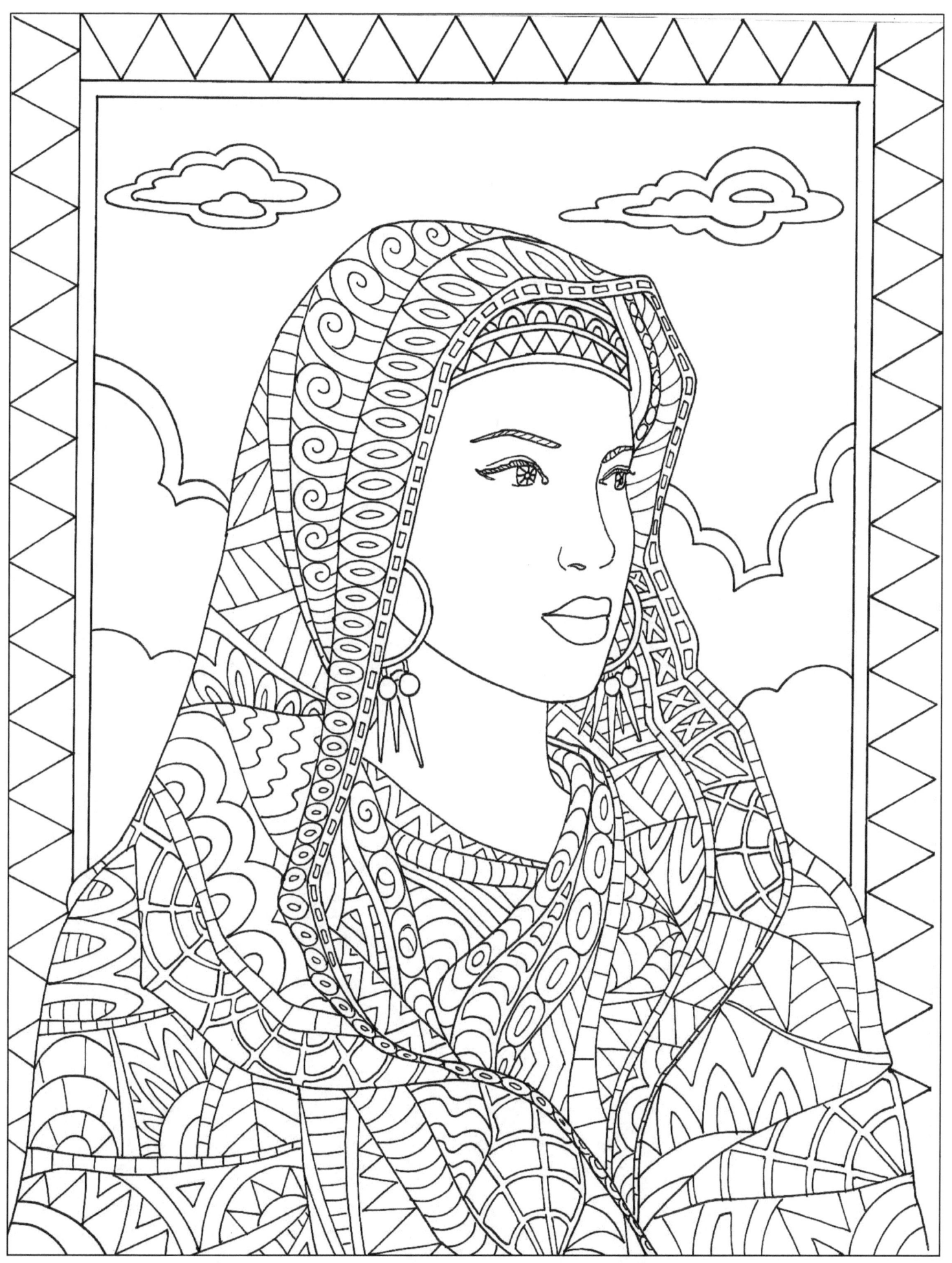

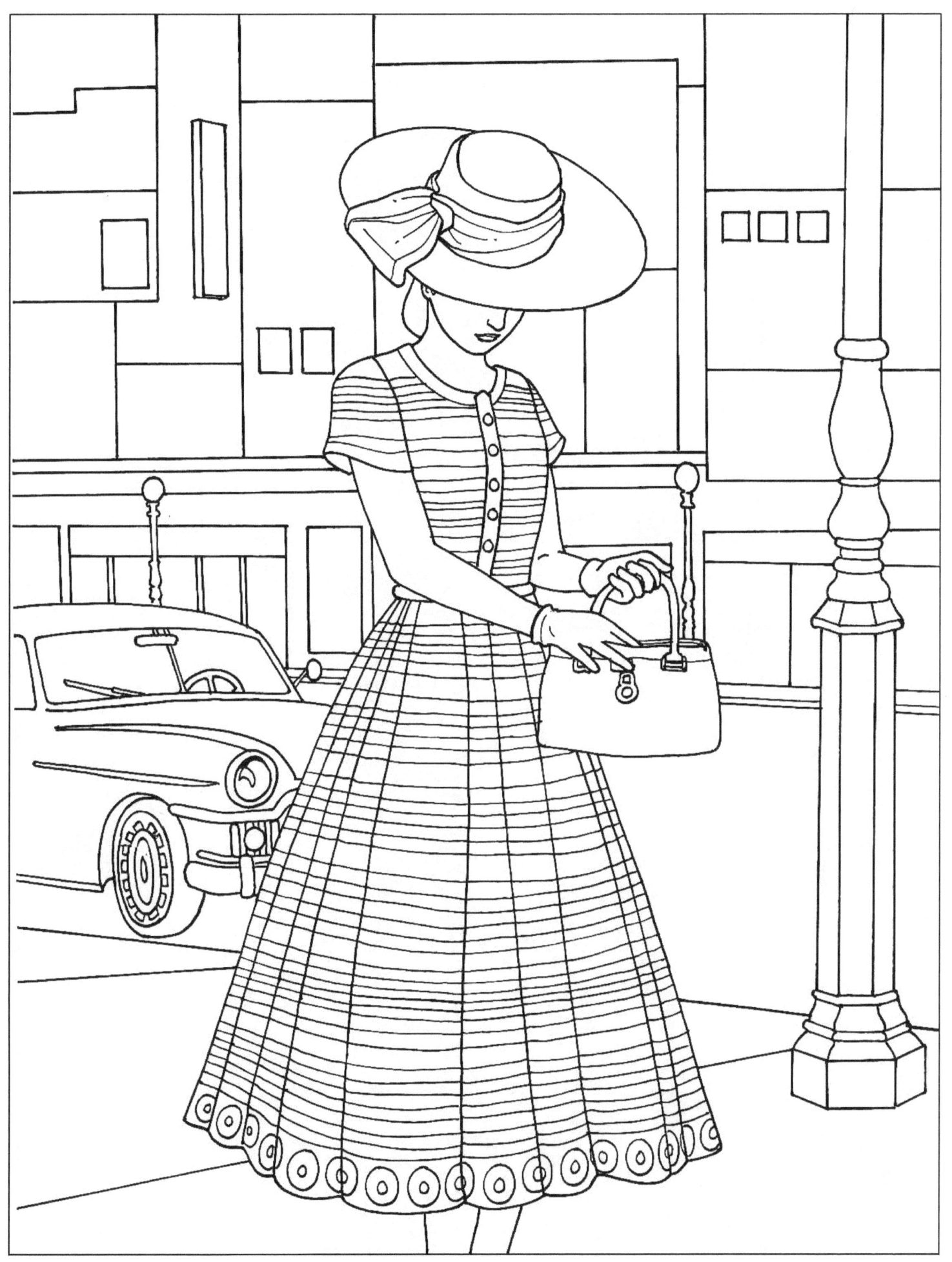

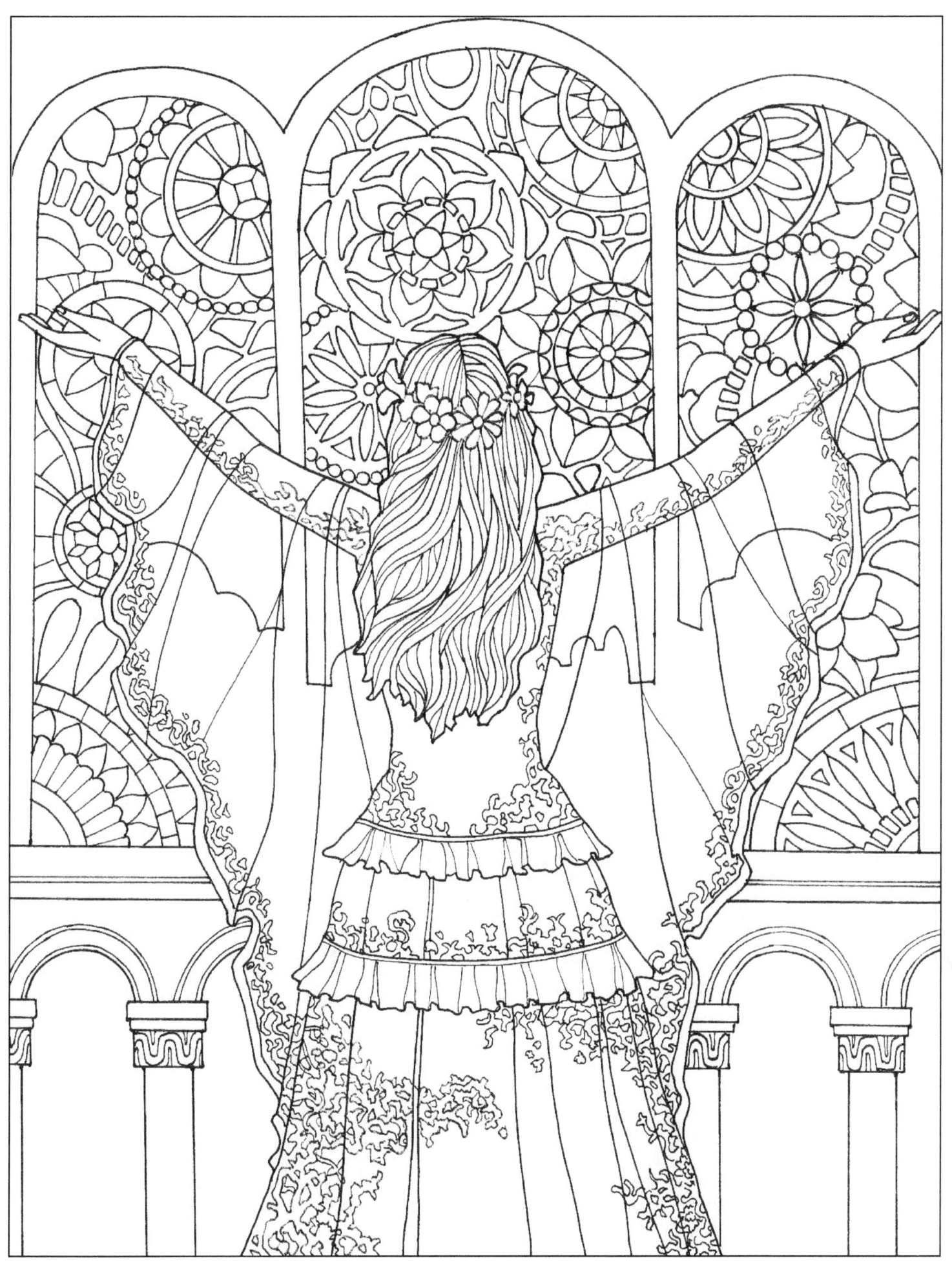

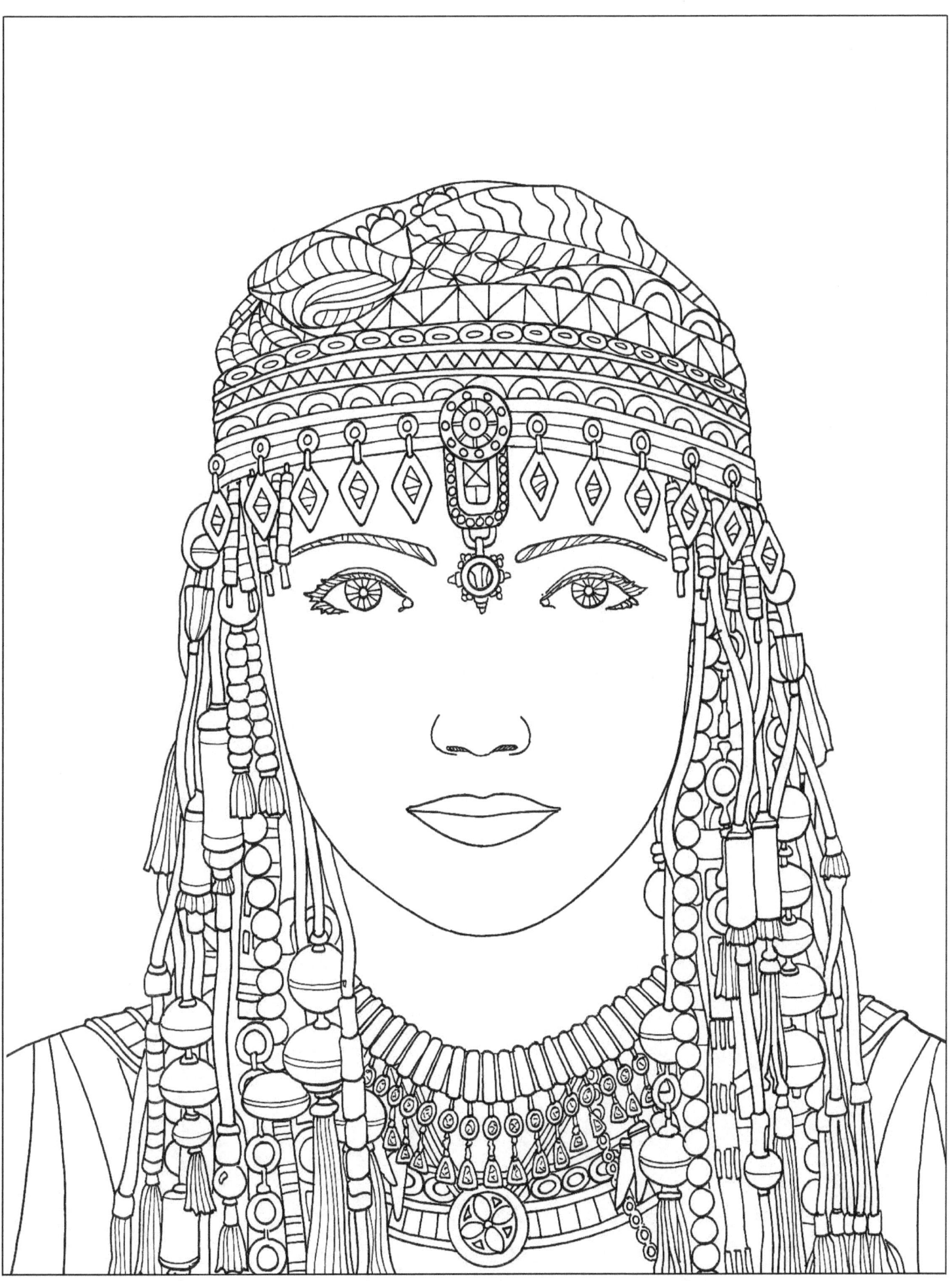

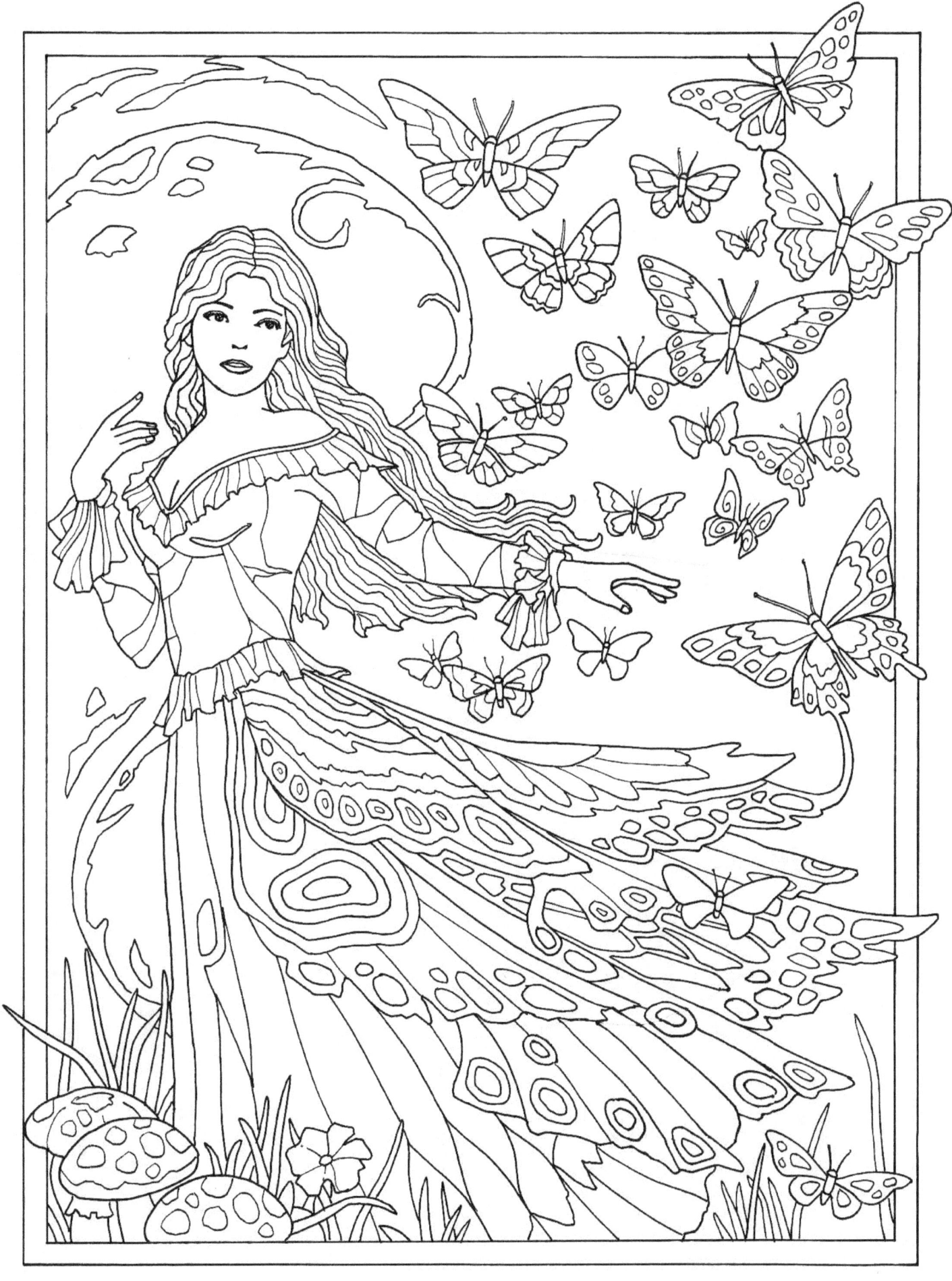

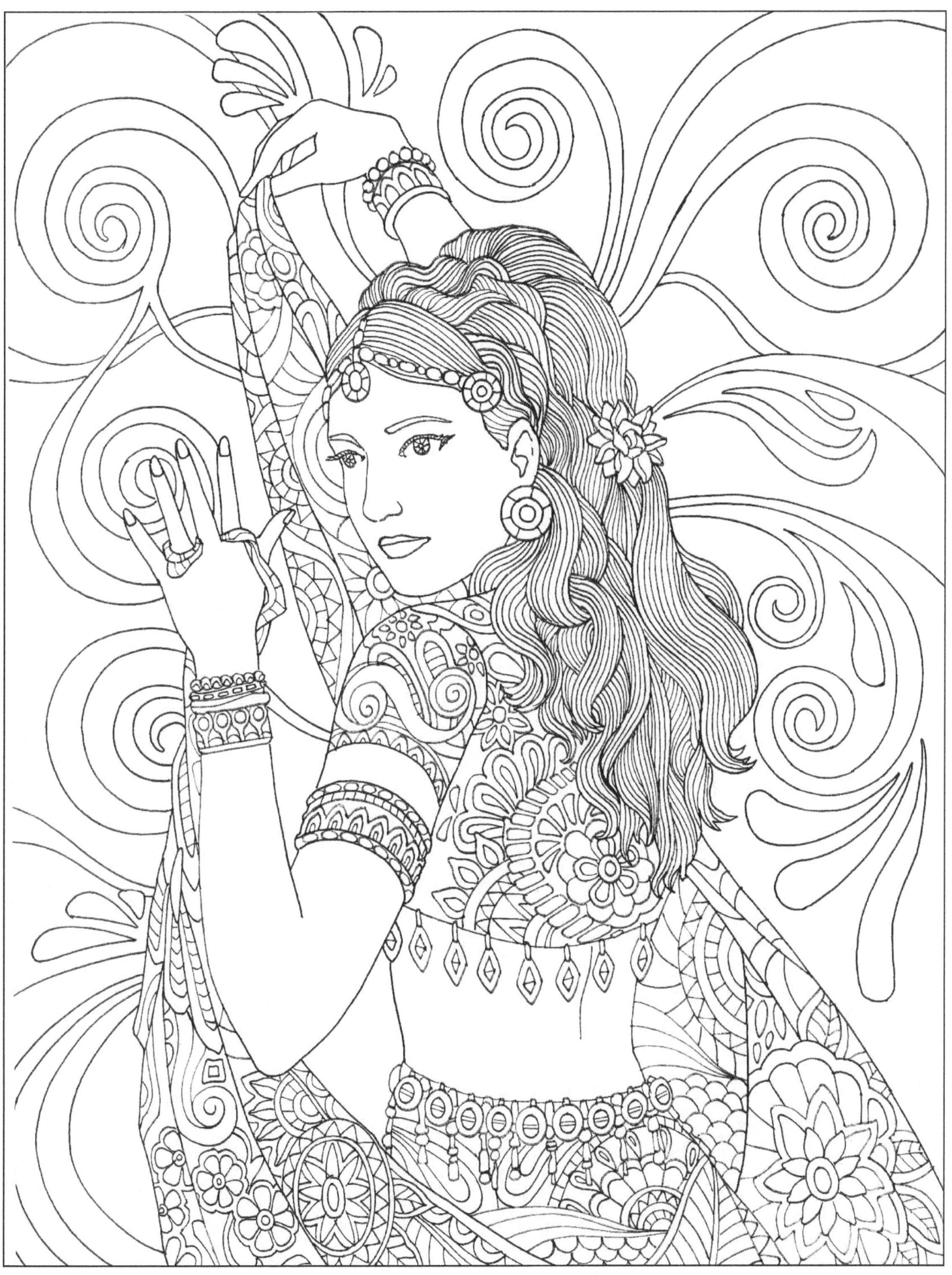

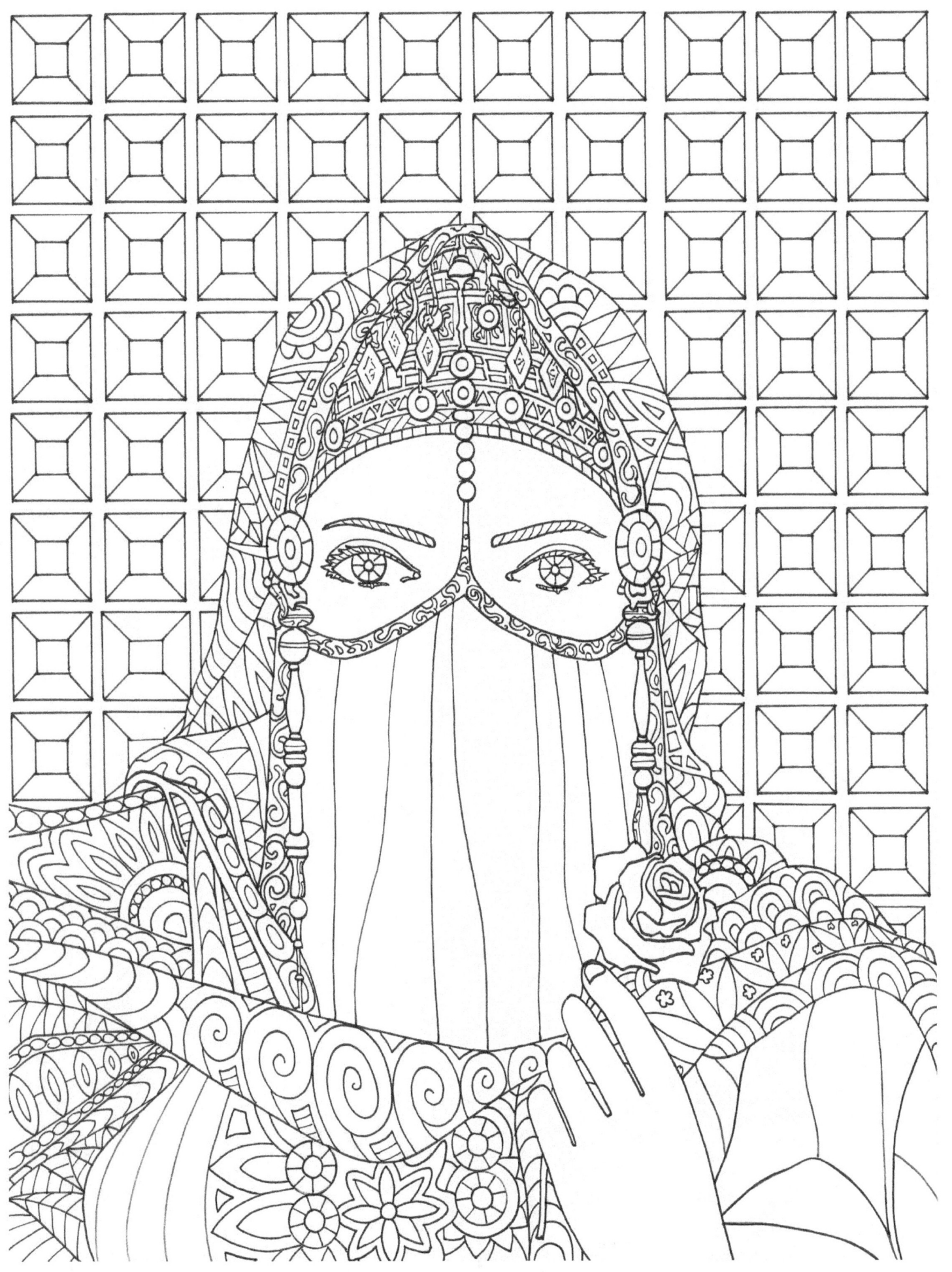

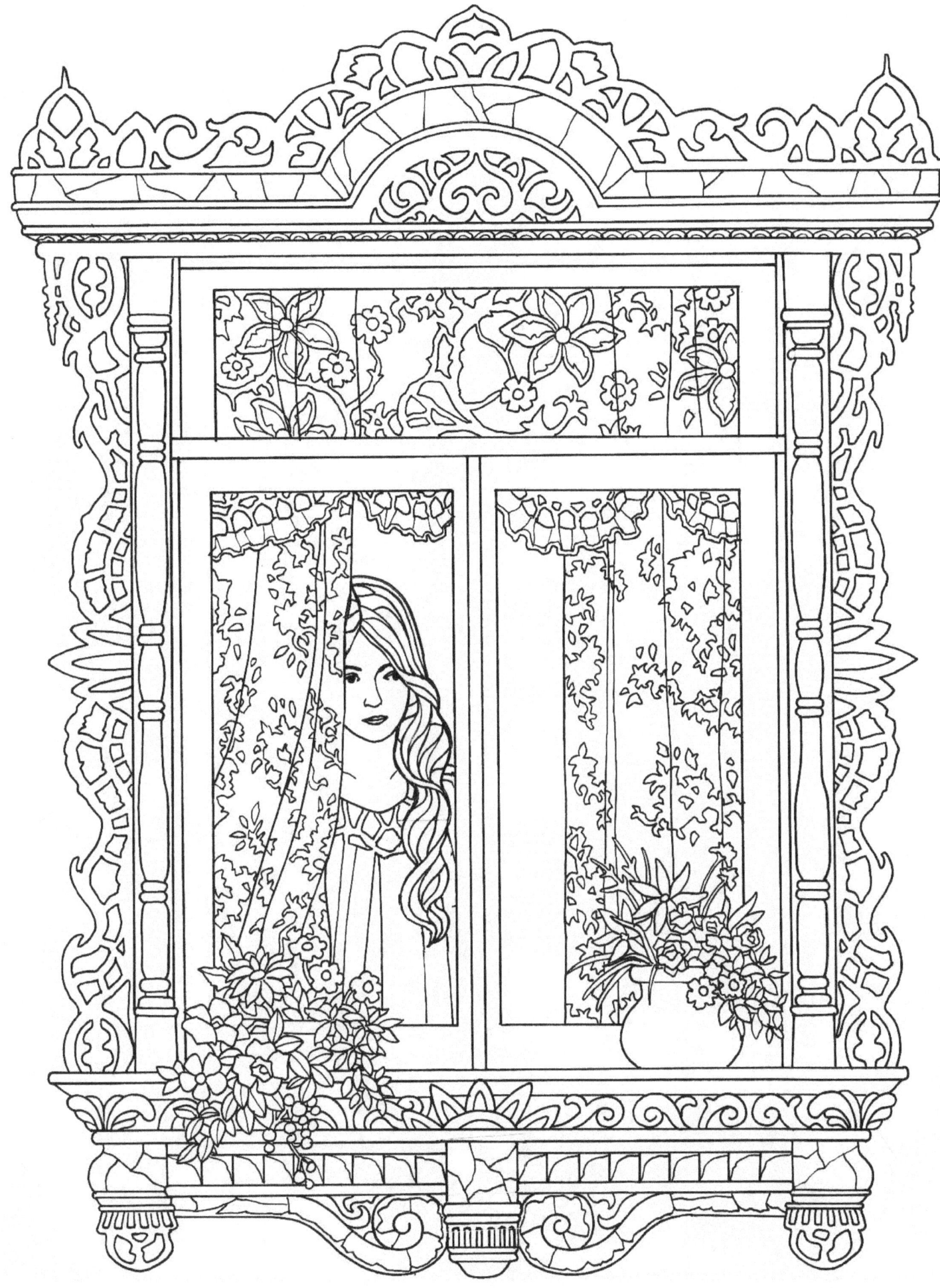

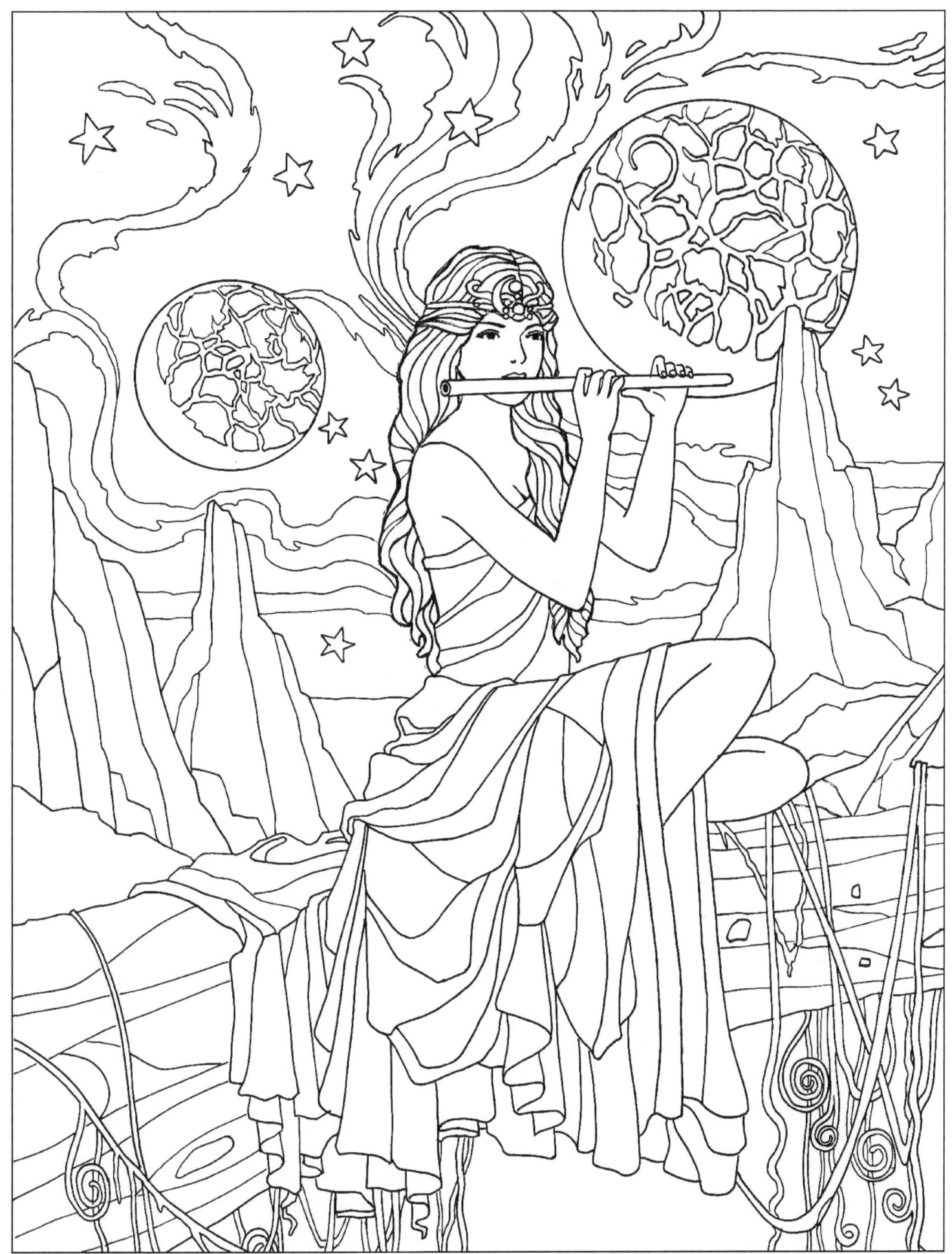

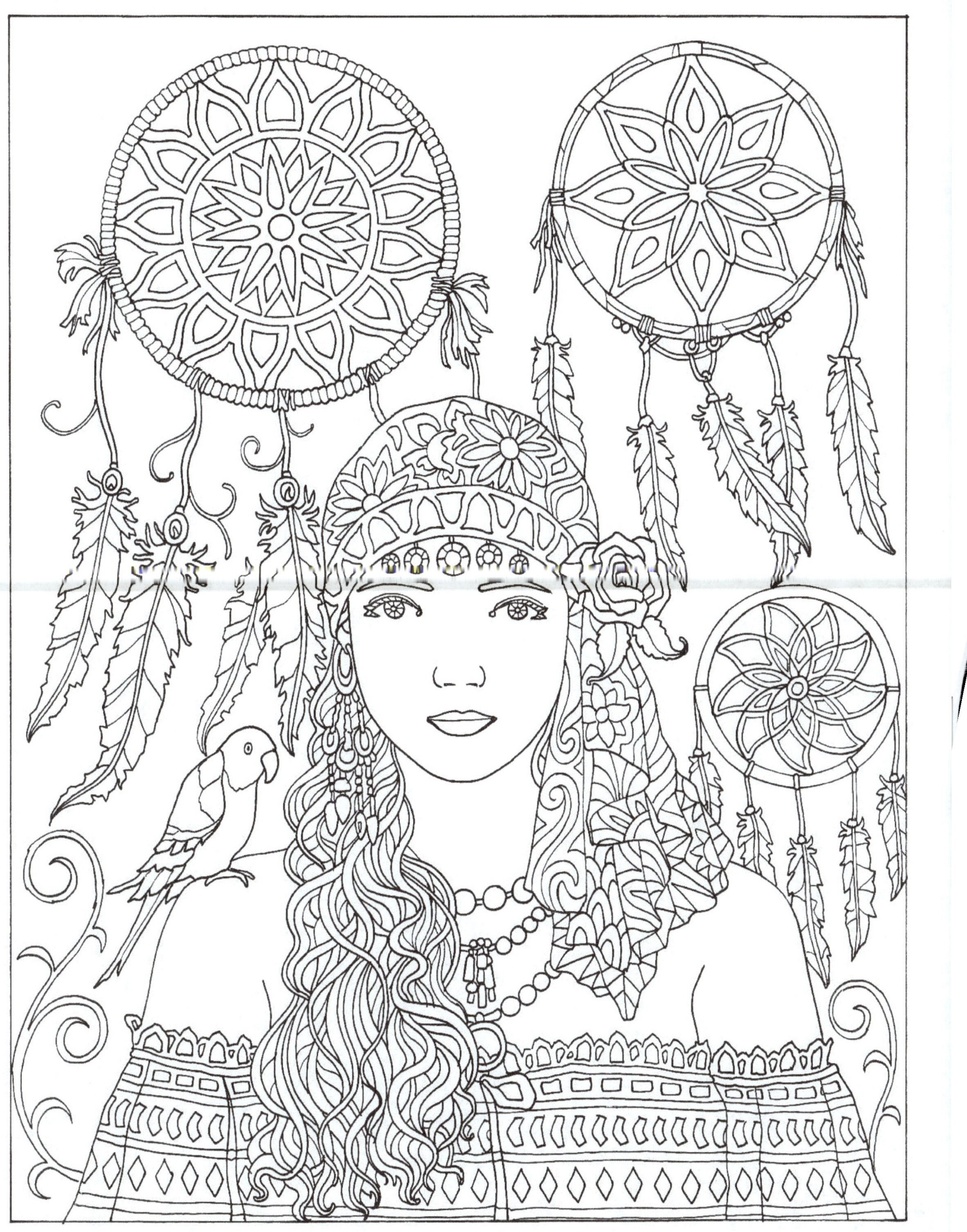